Joan

From one writer to another, Congratulations on your great book & the beautiful artist that you are. Most impressive.

with love
Russ Gallagher

PLACES

PLACES

THE JOURNEY OF MY DAYS, MY LIVES
THAAO PENGHLIS

Places
The Journey of My Days, My Lives

Copyright © 2014 Thaao Penghlis

First published in 2014 by Padaro Press.
An operating unit of Morling Manor Corporation
Los Angeles, California

All rights reserved. No part of this book may be reproduced or transmitted in any form or by any means, electronic or mechanical, including photocopying, recording, or by any information storage and retrieval system, without written permission from the publisher, except where permitted by law.

Print ISBN: 978-1-62467-256-9

For my dearest friend Jo De Winter
and my parents Peter and Eva
whose love really made a difference
and brought magic into my life

A special gratitude to Jack Betts who stood by my side and took so many of the wonderful photos that I have incorporated in this book which always allowed me to remember how fortunate I've been. Roy Steinberg for helping me create Journeys *at the Cape May Stage that seeded the idea for this book. To my dearest friend Jo De Winter for that incredible mind and all those wonderful arguments on history when the facts were not always clear. To Milton Katselas for inspiring me as a teacher and friend, who helped me as a fellow Greek understand the meaning of "mentor." A special thank you to Brian Nahas, for without him I would never have had the opportunity to meet my passionate and talented publisher Judy Proffer. That relationship introduced me to my editor Karen Young, who through her sincere work and valuable insights helped me believe in my voice. Thank you to Lauren Gibson, Terri Hanauer and Denise George for helping me put this book together. And finally my dear brother George Pengly and his wife Helen who contributed more than they will ever realize. My first book, a new experience that has placed more light on this continued path.*

CONTENTS

Part I.
Along the Path..17

Part II.
Dodging Bullets 51

Part III.
Places 73

FOREWORD

I've known Thaao Penghlis for over twenty years, sharing a master acting class every Saturday morning. Our teacher Milton Katselas taught the class at the Beverly Hills Playhouse and over the years I was fortunate to be in the audience when Thaao would work on the stage. I was witness to his talent, his inventiveness, the depth of his choices, and his unique style. He is a very serious actor who fills his characters with great detail. When he is onstage, it is his performance that you watch. There's always intelligence, clarity, drama, and originality to his work. In addition, a very handsome man!

Because of our friendship, I have been fortunate enough to be invited to his home several times for dinner. He's an extraordinary cook and takes great pleasure in inviting his friends to his home for an evening of great food, wine, and interesting conversation. The table is set so beautifully that you almost hate to sit down to mess it up! There's an elegance to it, a color scheme, attractive plates, lovely stemware, flowers, and always a comfortable chair. The food that he cooks takes his time, thoughtfulness and knowledge, and he spends hours preparing a very well-planned dinner, salad, dessert and, of course, wine. His guests are always interesting people and one is lucky to be among the chosen for a lovely, memorable, and delicious dinner. I am always grateful to be among the invited. Thaao's home is a delight for the eyes, filled with extraordinary art and antiques. There's always a feeling of warmth, comfort, and love in his house. He makes you feel all that at once.

It's during these meals that Thaao regales us with fascinating stories of his travels and adventures around the world. It is these stories that make up this book, full of insight from his personal life, his family heritage, and lessons learned by walking through history.

In this century Thaao Penghlis is a true renaissance man. A wonderful actor, a delicious cook, and now a fascinating author. His book is intriguing, informative, and an absolute page-turner. His life has been very interesting, his internationally renowned mentors have been influential in the wise choices he's made. Each page takes you on a journey and reveals illuminating experiences from his life and his travels, and makes this book a wonderfully unique experience.

—Doris Roberts

INTRODUCTION

"In every great religion in the world there is a place where God never sleeps, where the Divine and mundane connect and out of this comes revelation."
— Richard Marshall

From an early age I harbored an insatiable desire to explore mysterious places as gateways to profound spiritual awakening. Turkey. Egypt. Greece. Israel. Syria. Lebanon. Jordan. I never imagined that landing in America would set the stage for a lifetime of exploration. I *did* believe that the knowledge I would gain in traveling to these off-the-beaten-path places would lead to a better understanding of self and inch me closer to assuming the role I coveted most: "Captain of My Own Destiny."

So in my early twenties I was left to ponder what province could afford me the opportunity for dreams to become reality.

While exploring the merits of various vocations, including archeology and diplomacy, it was the acting profession that eventually came calling. Yes, it came to me. At least the *notion* of a career in acting. I had to work like crazy to earn the right to respectfully be part of the business. And once I broke through and established myself, the acting path and its rewards afforded me the opportunity to visit life-altering places.

So, travel I did.

I reveled in extraordinary journeys laced with mind-bending and soul-stirring adventures and experiences — crossing Egypt's Sinai Desert and climbing Mt. Moses; crashing in a balloon ride over the Valley of the Kings in Luxor; being mistaken for a terrorist by Mossad agents in Israel. I was (wrongly) accused of being an Israeli spy by the Hezbollah. I researched sixty thousand documents in Greece by archaeologist Heinrich Schliemann so I could better understand the footsteps he took in uncovering the remains of Troy. These experiences all added startling new dimension to my already rich perception of life's great big mysteries.

There are many stories to tell about my journeys — and in this book I have curated some of what I consider to be the best and most interesting to share with you.

Travel has always been and always will be my great big love. Sure, I've had my heart broken and I've likely broken hearts. What has shaped me more than anything else — romantically, intellectually and spiritually — are my adventures to distant lands. I hope you too will find the romance in the places I visited. I hope your heart and soul are stirred as mine have been again and again. The first rule of acting is to be real. I believe that applies to writing too. Travel is my greatest truth.

The roots of this book took form in 2010 when I created a theatre piece of my pilgrimages called *Journeys*. It was then I discovered that audiences were also curious and fascinated by what awaits beyond their shores. By sharing my revelations as a Homeric storyteller, I learned that I purposely stirred people with my explorations and inspired them to look beyond what may be considered the mundane.

I approach travel as a scholar, not as a tourist. I toss out a "must do" list in favor of studying and delving into the bones of a culture. Exploring and wearing the dust of these lands leaves an everlasting imprint on the psyche. This kind of travel changes the way you think, act, and feel. It holistically generates a fresh way of looking at the world by rejuvenating the way we live in our own space.

It was Henry Ward Beecher who once said, "We should not judge people by their peak of excellence; but by the distance they have traveled from the point where they started."

Not all paths taken are safe. Very few meaningful things are without risks. Acting is a risk. Relationships are risks. And so is travel to sometimes perilous lands.

Glimpsing into a new culture firsthand offers a clearer understanding of the ways people live and have lived throughout history. We gain a greater understanding of how our personal existence fits in with the global community. And if we do it right, if we completely immerse when we travel, we can unfurl compassion and keep criticism at bay and ultimately honor and accept the differences and similarities among us.

It was the rituals of daily life in Australia that grounded me — sitting at the dining table without the television on; kissing my father's hand on his Name Day; watching my grandmother crochet my sister's dowry; my mother disciplining me for speaking to an elder without respect; or her handing me a protein drink with a raw egg every morning so that I would grow taller — and finally, my brother George, who was always there at the end of a race, cheering me on.

I left my family to go to America. No one in my Greek community had ever left their family. I was the first and I put my family through a great deal of pain and confusion when I moved, especially my Mum. One relative spouted, "Actors, cab drivers, they're all the same." This opinion prompted me to push through toward my career and look for signs along the way that I had made the right decision — always remaining connected to my family.

My Mum was royalty in my eyes. She would sit with her friends, always with her head held high. My father was tough and judgmental, but I would later learn that his heart was in the right place — he was a product of his background and just didn't know how to show it.

My parents were among tens of thousands who emigrated from Greece to Australia in the first half of the 20th century. I cherish their memory and all those who came before them who took the chance to go to Australia when there was so little to grasp in those lean years. They carved roads on the hard Australian soil, and challenged what lay ahead by persevering and believing. They cleared the path for all of us.

My Greek roots and passion led me on these journeys, navigating my own personal path through the darkness and the light. Oftentimes challenging, the path I took led me to where I am today.

Acclaimed spiritual teacher and author Marianne Williamson once said, "Our deepest fear is not that we are inadequate. Our deepest fear is that we are powerful beyond measure. It is our light, not our darkness that most frightens us. And when we let our light shine we unconsciously give other people permission to do the same. As we are liberated from our own fear our presence automatically liberates others."

Through it all, my life so far has been a great ride — with many more adventures to come. If this diary encourages you to rethink travel, mission accomplished. And to those who crossed my path, thank you for making a difference in the way I see, feel, and am.

The beginning of unraveling the mysteries of self. First photograph taken in America, 1969. (Photo: Edgar De Evia)

Sydney in the late '60s. (Author's Collection)

I. ALONG THE PATH

Sydney

It was the late '60s. I was seated at my desk in the Commonwealth Center where I was an Immigration Official interviewing candidates for permanent status in Australia when a curious man with an even more curious name sat down before me.

Marinus B. Dykshoorn. He told me he was a psychic who solved crimes with Scotland Yard. His soothsaying career spanned decades and his cases spanned Europe. And apparently he was a bit of a legend in psychic circles. Born in 1920 in a small Dutch town, he first gained notoriety by insisting an infertile neighbor had a "baby in her tummy." Nine months later the young boy's prediction was vindicated. In Belgium he unearthed the remains of seven soldiers buried during World War I. And his clairvoyance would draw him to a bounty of silver coins buried during World War II. His memoir was titled *My Passport Says Clairvoyant*. Because it did.

Dykshoorn came to the Commonwealth Center to discuss his status, and by the end of our meeting the discussion turned toward me. With unwavering conviction he told me I would not be working at my job much longer and that I would be moving to America to become an actor. I stared at him in utter disbelief. My dream was to work in the Diplomatic Corps. It seemed to me a noble career and frankly it met with my parents' approval.

Wary of his "vision" but curious as hell, I agreed to meet with Dykshoorn privately three days later. What transpired in that exchange would alter my life forever. He held a wire whisk in his hands, spinning it until he was able to pick up vibrations around me, deciphering them as he went along. This was a completely new experience because I never had a session with a psychic before.

Dykshoorn told me that on the 29th of August that year I would fly on a free trip to America and begin studies as an actor. He also said my biggest success would be portraying Machiavellian characters. Stunned, I thanked him and headed home absolutely elated by his predictions.

My family responded to my news with a numb silence. When they eventually shared their thoughts, they were shocked that I would even contemplate such a frivolous scenario. Influenced by their response, I dropped the idea as quickly as I had first accepted it and kept working with the Immigration Department.

My next post was meeting immigrants aboard ships entering Sydney Harbor filled with single Greek women on assisted passage. At 5 a.m. I would catch the launch with a couple of fellow officers and speed out to the heads, climb on board the ship and complete documents for these young women entering the labor force.

One morning everyone from my office missed the launch and I had to interview five hundred women on my own within a period of two hours. I saved the day since this could have proven embarrassing for the government if word had leaked to the press. The head official called me into his office and congratulated me on a job well done, and elevated me to a position that normally took ten years of seniority. He told me I was the first Greek who was ever trusted there.

"What was wrong with the others?" I asked.

"They took bribes," was his matter-of-fact reply.

At that point Dykshoorn's predictions were a distant memory and I contentedly continued with my work. I was a young Greek living in Australia and I would make the most of my life. One evening I was invited to a party where Amelia Hernandez of the famed Ballet Folklórico of Mexico was the featured guest.

She was gracious and passionate and said I reminded her of her favorite son. Amelia was greatly interested in my classical Greek heritage and shared with me how Greek history influenced her choreography. As she was leaving the party Amelia surprised me with an invitation to join her on a trip to Mexico.

"Come and see how my country lives and play with us. It won't cost you anything as we are on a chartered flight and you will be our guest."

My curiosity was naturally piqued and I asked when the flight was leaving.

"On the 29th of August," she replied.

Dykshoorn's date.

She gave me her number in case I was interested. I rushed home to share the news. Once again, talk of America was met with gloom and doom. My parents summoned relatives for a family discussion on the prospect of my heading far away to become an actor.

"You have a good profession here and no good Greek boy would leave his family before getting married" was the consensus. My mother was worried. I quietly agreed. Or so they thought.

I alone knew I was about to fly away from Australia with untested wings, regardless of my family's objections.

I called Amelia and accepted her proposal. And then took a leave of absence from the department for a year. After things were irrevocably in motion I shared my decision with the family, which left them flabbergasted. My mother couldn't stop crying and my father was brutal in his opposition.

The sole voice of support was that of my Uncle Bill, who above the protest shouted "Let him go, and if it all comes true for him, we will all be happy, and if not at least he gave it a try."

It was his faith that allowed me to leave Australia with a degree of hope. But as I boarded the plane on the 29th of August, fear crept in and traveled through my body as I looked out to my anxious parents and siblings. I wondered if the rest of Dykshoorn's predictions could come true.

For the first time in my life I was alone.

I visited Mexico City for a couple of weeks. I was on a budget and the accommodations were fine, but no one warned me about the water. I knew a little Spanish since I had studied it for six months back in Oz. The cuisine was new to me, and I willingly sampled the culinary riches of the region. Machaca, a tender meat dish, was my favorite and I loved the crust. Like the Greeks make. The aroma was distinctly Mexican. It's the smell of corn.

Amelia and her troupe were incredibly generous with their time. I was given a tour of the city and visited the Teotihuacán and Chichén Itzá pyramids. Even though I had dreamed of first seeing the Pyramids at Giza, Egypt, these structures were simply amazing. And being amidst such greatness deepened my hunger to visit Giza. Little did I know that in my future I would eventually visit Egypt on ten separate occasions.

This journey to North America would become the stepping-stone for all my discoveries both physically and metaphysically in my life. I loved the people in Mexico who crossed my path and will always remember them as my first introduction to a foreign culture. It was the gateway to the United States, where I was headed next.

Sitting on top of the highest pyramid in the Yucatán. (Author's Collection)

New York

I landed in New York City in September of 1967 with $180 in my pocket. I stayed with a friend from Australia, but was asked to leave after a couple of weeks. Apparently my rich buddy from back home was a bit of a snob and only dealt with what he considered to be the "great minds" of New York. So much for country. So much for friendship. Years later, after my success, he apologized for his abhorrent behavior. By then it was too late. I had made it on my own, and frankly I found *him* to be a bore. And I told him just that. Turning me out on the street was a cruel act. I knew no one else there, and it was easy to lose your way in New York, figuratively and literally. It was an awakening, and I never depended on any friend since.

I felt lost, but as luck would have it I was able to secure a position at the Australian Mission to the UN where I worked as a secretary, answering phone calls for the Ambassador, who was constantly drunk.

I thought it was a disgrace.

Calls would come in and I would find him collapsed on the toilet. I knew my time would be limited there. It had to be. I was looking for a mentor, some guiding factor that would help me stay on course.

At first, the city was scary, but once I got in sync with the rhythm and energy of the place I was able to handle its demands. It's never a happy time when you're broke and living in New York City. I lived in a studio apartment on 33rd and 2nd. The place was so small it gave me nightmares. But in my mind I lived in a villa and knew my hovel was only a temporary residence.

I told my parents that I was only going away for three weeks, and now it was a year later and my mother was pretty much beside herself. My father was running out of excuses for my absence, and so the rumors began.

"He is probably over there doing drugs and whoring around. Why else wouldn't he be back here where he belongs?"

"He's a cab driver, what else do these poor actors do?"

Well, I was living in New York where at times I could only afford an apple for dinner or a tin of ravioli. I would save for three months to buy a new shirt. I thought of my family often, how could I not? I missed the Australian meat pie, the aroma of my mother's sweets and the earthiness of Greek peasant cooking — including calf's brain with capers. When I would find Greek delicacies, not easy to come by, they were too expensive. Not on my piece-of-fruit-for-dinner budget. But in my head I was living a bigger life. And every once in a while I got a glimpse of New York grandeur.

One evening I was invited to an exclusive and expensive social gathering. A contact from Australia had suggested that I call upon some friends of his from Scotland, experts in ancient art. He thought we'd have something in common. I hesitated at first because of my shyness. But I was lonely. So I forced myself to make the call. I could not afford to buy even the smallest gift for the hostess. A tin of ravioli is not exactly New York chic no matter how you dress it up. And I hated the thought of showing up empty-handed (a nod to my Greek upbringing), so I strolled over to Park Avenue and cut some tulips that were growing along the center of the avenue. A perfectly normal thing to do, right? I looked upon it as my own garden and selected a dozen pristine white blooms, carefully wrapped them in newspaper and carried them to the cocktail party.

The hostess purred with gratitude and asked where I found such a striking bouquet.

"Oh, over on Park Avenue."

I'm not certain if she was amused or appalled, but assuming she was amused, it was a great lesson on how to charm New York elite with just pennies in your pocket.

And what a great night that was.

During the evening I was introduced to an art dealer by the name of James Goldie, an expert in the field of Chinese and English 18th-century art. His business partner was Robert Ellsworth, at the time America's leading expert in Southeast Asian sculpture.

Perhaps due to my accent and fairly vast knowledge of English history, James offered me a job as an apprentice in their gallery at seventy-five dollars a week. I accepted and gladly left the Australian Mission.

Ellsworth would have me read chapters upon chapters on the incoming inventory daily in order to make myself very familiar with their collection. Museums and private collectors were their clientele — and by appointment only.

I loved walking through the gallery and sitting upon the only 18th-century Queen Anne sofas in the United States. The gallery housed the best collection of Southeast Asian sculpture in America. I was surrounded by works of exemplary beauty and enjoyed immersing my mind into the books and art in order to gain more knowledge.

Claudette, Andy and Jackie

It was the end of my first year at Ellsworth and Goldie when just before lunch Ellsworth escorted the wonderful Claudette Colbert into the gallery. She was the first "star" I ever met. She must have been in her mid-60s at the time.

Growing up in Australia I watched Miss Colbert in many of her movies. She was graceful without any attitude, unlike Ellsworth who always had his nose stuck in the air.

After I stood to meet her, she smiled to Ellsworth and said, "Oh, Robert, please bring Thaao to lunch with us…he is so pretty."

Ellsworth quickly dismissed the idea, saying I was needed to hold court in the gallery since his partner Goldie was out of town. Disappointed, I reluctantly bowed out but only after telling her, "It would have been a pleasure."

After they left I noticed a shoebox that Miss Colbert had left behind, and seized both the shoebox and the opportunity to be in her magnetic presence once again. I closed up the shop and hurried to the French restaurant down the street. As I walked in I caught the eye of Ellsworth, who was staring at me furiously. He didn't stand up. He rarely did. He loved every throne he ever sat in.

He immediately demanded, "What are you doing here? And who's minding the shop?"

I ignored him, turned to Miss Colbert and said, "Madam, you forgot this and I thought it might be important."

She unleashed a big smile and said, "Oh, Robert, he is so sweet, let him stay for lunch."

A pointed "No!" was his definitive response. No room for negotiation.

Disappointed yet again, I left to guard the shop. I called my family to share the story of meeting a Hollywood legend. I felt it was a sign I was on my way. Everyone was genuinely enthused to hear of my brush with Miss Colbert, but the dominating question remained: When would I come home?

"Soon, soon," I replied as always, appeasing them with shallow words, though my intentions were to stay in America and find my way. Somehow.

As I hung up the phone I noted a lanky pale figure checking his reflection in the glass window. He retrieved a comb and began to straighten his wayward but brilliant white locks. He stared into the window's exterior and couldn't see me inside because of the afternoon sun. I suddenly realized it was artist and filmmaker Andy Warhol. I wished I'd had a film camera on me as I observed this unique artist having a private moment of vanity. Or was it insecurity? Satisfied that everything was in place, he disappeared. Warhol was known for outlandish creativity and doing things his way. Was this a sign to forge ahead with my own alleged destiny? Or simply a glimpse into the life of a man whose shock of hair was a victim of a windy New York afternoon? And then a sinking thought crossed my mind: Could it be that I would always be on the inside looking out?

Sitting despondently at my desk, a knock on the door brought me out of my self-imposed stupor. As all visits were scheduled in advance, I rose to turn away whoever was interrupting my melancholy reflections.

I opened the door to say, "Sorry, appointments only," and was astonished to see American history standing before me: An elegant Jacqueline Kennedy was apologizing for showing up without an appointment. I was elated but kept my composure. She told her two bodyguards to remain outside while she explored the gallery. I asked her if she would like some tea, and surprisingly she graciously accepted.

I quickly called upstairs to Masahiro, the Japanese houseman, and instructed him to make tea for a special guest.

He laughed and scoffed, "You joking. Apprentice like you not order such a thing, and with Ellsworth's best silver? You crazy?"

As Mrs. Kennedy walked past the elevator, the door suddenly opened, revealing Masahiro standing in shorts. When he saw her he gasped, "Oh, my God," placed his hands over his mouth and repeatedly bowed in apology. The doors closed as I escorted our distinguished guest to the back of the gallery to a room three stories high filled with the best private collection of Southeast Asian sculpture in the world.

The ceiling was made of glass and was designed to reflect the changing light of the New York skyline. It was still grey outside, making the large studio seem like a tomb. It was all meticulously lit by Ellsworth, who had a brilliant eye. Every piece told a story. Arrogant as he was, the man had phenomenal taste and was a greatly respected expert in his field.

Mrs. Kennedy sat in her element, coaxing me to tell her the origins of the ancient pieces. Masahiro brought a lavish tray filled with afternoon delights and tea. He must have raided the safe. Dressed in his proper costume along with his cool Asian manner, he poured the tea. As he was leaving he looked my way with scorn and envy as if to say, *You lucky bastard.*

I spent an hour with Jacqueline Kennedy. The knowledge I accumulated under Ellsworth's direction was priceless. I told her that the Chinese always believed that the spirit of the artist was with their creation forever. That was something I had picked up from him during the "seduction" of a potential buyer. They were rare pieces from Vietnam, China and Japan dating from the Han period of the 2nd century BC to the Ming Dynasty in the 16th century AD.

As I joined her for tea, she inquired about my Greek heritage. I expounded upon the subject and spoke passionately about the culture from which I had escaped. She appeared to be really interested, an eager student of life.

She was beautifully dressed with that famous pillbox hat and possessed a truly sophisticated manner. It was easy to see why she had been a First Lady and was so greatly admired by her country. Our exchange took place in only one hour, but the timing was extraordinary, and it furthered my belief that I hadn't made a mistake coming to New York. For the first time, I had a sense of success because I no longer felt like that Greek immigrant from Australia looking for the right path.

When Robert Ellsworth returned from lunch alone, he asked me if anyone important had called or come in.

"Yes, Jacqueline Kennedy," I said, beaming.

He kept walking up the stairs, mocking me. "Sure, sure, sure."

That day went along quietly until Ellsworth called me up to his office to tell me that the purpose of Miss Colbert's visit was the need to duplicate two paintings, an Utrillo and a Monet. He said that the humidity in her Barbados home was beginning to damage her art. Over the next month I would watch both paintings come to life, and to the naked eye you could not tell the difference. The fakes were amazing. The originals were sold off at Christie's and the fakes hung in her home, and no one knew until her death when her estate claimed them as the forgeries that they were.

Meanwhile, a call came in from Jacqueline Kennedy, interested in a head sculpture from China that I had shown her. To Ellsworth's surprise — and dismay — she was only interested in speaking with me. He bantered on about who he was and how he was more equipped to handle the transaction. The former First Lady insisted on talking to the apprentice. And only the apprentice. His ego badly bruised, Ellsworth handed me the phone with contempt. I had my first sale.

Three weeks later Jacqueline Kennedy married Aristotle Onassis. The joke among my family and friends was that she had to meet up with another Greek to make up her mind to marry the shipping tycoon.

My time with Ellsworth and Goldie was ultimately cut short because soon after that spectacular first sale they announced the breakup of their partnership. I was sorry to hear that news, as up to that point it was the greatest piece of education I'd ever had. The knowledge imparted by Ellsworth still resonates with me today.

Goldie died a number of years ago, but Ellsworth is in his 80s and wheelchair-bound. The last thing I heard was that his great art collection was to be auctioned off at Christie's.

Redford, Gielgud and Evans

I was blessed to have had those experiences in art and antiques and to learn as much as I did. But I wondered where the acting career was that Dykshoorn had predicted. I was determined to stay in the States and found my next employer — working with the renowned men's fashion designer Roland Meledandri. He had a stellar reputation for quality, and his sophisticated shop on 56th Street in Manhattan was a gathering place for the art and entertainment world in the '60s and '70s.

I was in my twenties when we met, and Roland offered me a job on the spot. He liked the way I dressed and the way I sounded. He said I was ideal for the atmosphere he created. So I accepted and soon found myself working with producers and actors and, once again, New York's elite.

Meledandri had a reputation for being very high-strung. He was known to break coat hangers in fits of rage. Our relationship had a great connection based on trust, and after a short time he gave me permission to work the register, a big deal in the Meledandri world as he was preternaturally distrusting.

Ralph Lauren had worked for him, and they began to form a partnership designing ties, but that failed when the Polo label was established and Ralph Lauren went on to become the legend he is today. I believe Roland was bitter. And that seed planted his inability to trust.

One time a regular customer came in to pick up a $3,000 suit, and two days later he returned, seething. I was the one who had given him his final fitting, and when I questioned him about the alleged issue with the suit, the customer flew into a rage. I knew that no finished product ever left the premises short of perfection. That was Roland's style, and here his work and integrity were being questioned.

The customer stood in front of the mirror criticizing the tailoring. It suddenly occurred to me that he had gone elsewhere, had had it altered, and come back to ridicule Roland in front of his customers. I whispered my assumption in Roland's ear. He just stared at me in shock that someone would do this.

I noticed that when the customer went to change he had taken some shirts and a briefcase in with him. When he came out in a huff I suspected he was also a thief as the merchandise was no longer in the dressing room. I unlocked his case when he wasn't looking. He argued with Roland about never coming back, and as he lifted his case to leave, three shirts and a sweater fell out. Roland quietly told him to leave. The other customers were in shock, while the red-faced thief exited. I was embraced for revealing the truth.

One day Robert Evans, the outspoken head of Paramount Studios at the time, came in for a fitting. He had the most feminine walk I had ever seen. He would sashay in with great attitude. With the tailor present, and while gazing in the mirror, the legendary spoiled kid from Brooklyn proceeded to rip off the temporary sleeves. He said the tailoring was an insult to his eye. Evans threw what was left of the jacket on the floor and walked out.

Roland was at lunch when this drama occurred, and when he returned told me pointedly that because it took place under my watch I had to make it right. Nervously, I called the producer's office. I hadn't even started in the entertainment business and now I was in trouble with the head of Paramount Studios.

So I went for the truth and explained, "Robert, it's just a suit; it's not as if it's as significant as the great movies that you have produced. Come in and we'll have a private session with the tailor, and I give you my word you'll walk out of here with perfection."

He was convinced. I now realize that that training helped me deal with those ego-based tyrants who lord over the entertainment industry. Some you like, some you don't. I appreciated Evans — he was a perfectionist and made some of the most brilliant films of the '70s, including *The Godfather* and *Chinatown*. He came in aloof, but when he left, Evans was his charming self — and so was Roland.

Robert Redford was also a regular customer. His production office was conveniently located above us. He would walk in with a cold attitude and ask if Roland was in. On three occasions my reply was "No, but..." and Redford would walk out without further response. I didn't find him to be the warmest individual, but then again he was an important star who had no time for small talk.

After getting advice from Roland I deployed a different tactic the next time Redford stepped halfway in.

"Oh, Mr. Redford, a beautiful suit just came in, and Mr. Meledandri insists that you try it on."

He paused and then asked if anyone else was on the premises. I said no, then locked the door behind him, which he seemed to appreciate. Redford had great style and a wonderful talent. He was just not an easy person to approach, and that was okay with me.

I was twenty-six at the time and my head kept screaming *Fuck, it's Robert Redford!*

I appeared calm, keeping my excitement at bay. I pulled out a brown velvet suit with ivory buttons that made my idol smile. He tried on the jacket that complemented his fair complexion perfectly. The usual routine was to slide your hands down the sides of the suit to give the feel of Meledandri's fine cut. High-cut armpits and a button placed right on the stomach gave the client the illusion of being taller while cutting down on any protruding shape. That was his genius.

But as I touched the sides of Redford I came across a pair of love handles and swiftly said, "If you want to wear this, you must lose all this." I grabbed his excess.

At that moment his mouth dropped open, as did mine for my unbelievable audacity.

Such a mouth, I thought.

He stared back at me, and after the initial shock dissipated, he flashed that spectacular Redford smile and said "You're absolutely right," and then broke into a laugh.

I remained a fan ever since, and happily for me Redford bought the suit. Ten years later at La Scala in Beverly Hills I spotted him sitting with Paul Newman. What a sight, to see the two of them together. La Scala was no stranger to Hollywood wattage, but this pairing was the mother lode. As they were leaving, Redford stopped by my table to say hello. My friends from Australia slipped into shock. "You know Robert Redford?"

"Yes, I do, but it's a long story."

One rainy morning Lillian Gish, the great silent screen star, came in to buy a gift for one of her dearest friends. She described him as a tall slim actor, and together they would celebrate his birthday in the South of France. She eventually selected a lovely pale blue silk shirt that I recommended, and we had it wrapped beautifully.

Two days later a Rolls-Royce pulled up outside Meledandri. Curious, I watched with Roland from the window. A cane popped out first and then a big hat.

What an entrance, I thought. Must be someone important.

As the passenger lifted his face up I realized it was Sir John Gielgud. And under his arm — unwrapped — was the gift I had recommended to Miss Gish.

Roland looked at me and said, "You take care of this one."

Nervously, I approached the door to open it, but Sir Gielgud beat me to it.

Out came that amazing voice bellowing through the store. "Where's Thaao?"

"Speaking," I said.

"Pale blue?" he admonished.

Facing me was the highly distinguished and prolific performer of the classics, considered to be one of the greatest actors of the 20th century. He was slightly imperious; after all, his accomplishments were immense. And here I was talking to him about a blue shirt. I quickly retreated from my awe and masked my reverence by displaying a number of other colors of the same shirt. He was pleased and chose a navy blue.

While he waited for it to be wrapped, he leaned on the counter and spoke to me like an old friend. I was impressed with his demeanor and felt incredibly privileged. He wanted to know about my dreams. When I told him I aspired to be an actor, he said that to fulfill the acting dream I must work hard and persevere.

"Acting," he said, was "a great privilege… You must earn it, and if fulfilled, it was a blessing from the gods."

He left and I was ecstatic. And so was Roland for my correcting the situation. I was inspired to discover that "great" privilege firsthand and fulfill my destiny.

Learning To Act

My first acting class was taught by Mary Tarcai. She was one of the first to teach classes centering on cold readings. I was there as an observer, but that didn't mean a thing to her. I was thrown when she asked me to read a scene in front of the class.

"No excuses," she said as I reluctantly got up. She blurted, "Let's see what you're made of."

With an abundance of fear and no preparation, I sat in a chair and shared the scene with another actor.

When the scene was over, she pulled no punches. "Why on Earth do you want to be an actor? I couldn't tell the difference between you and the chair."

I wanted to explain to her that I was new to acting, but she wasn't interested.

"Just sit down and listen," she said in a bewildered tone.

When I sat back in the class a young actress whispered, "Don't worry, honey, you're pretty."

For the first time I felt humiliated in America, and all I wanted to do was go home and forget about a business that did not come from my heart but from a psychic's prediction. I felt it was over, but I kept thinking about what Gielgud had said about perseverance. So I stuck it out for the next two years until I got the hang of it while still working for Meledandri.

Mary said my improvement was remarkable, and I began to see it myself and came to really love it. She became a good friend, and I was deeply saddened when she died in September 1979. She was my first acting teacher and the one who cleared my path — and that I will never forget. It's those tough ones that really made the difference.

With Milton in the late '70s. (Author's Collection)

The Katselas Years

My life changed when I met Milton Katselas in the early '70s. Our paths first crossed when a dear friend, the singer Sylvia Syms, took me backstage to meet him when he was directing Al Pacino in Tennessee Williams' *Camino Real* at Lincoln Center. He took an instant dislike to me. He believed I was arrogant and a dilettante. He had a great acting class, but he was not interested in my attending.

"But we're both Greeks, we're supposed to help each other," I said angrily. That was a myth that was smashed quickly, that we Greeks would look out for one another.

One day I saw Milton walking along the theatre district and I raced over to him. Again he said no.

"Well, let me observe," I implored, and he still said no and walked away.

So I chased after him again, and by the time I finished explaining my struggling story from Australia, he finally relented and said, "You come to my class but only temporarily for six months. It's a trial and I don't want a peep out of you."

Well, the lesson in persistence worked. Thanks, Sir John, for that advice. It was a year later and Milton was beginning his film career after a very successful run of *The*

Zoo Story and *Butterflies Are Free* on Broadway. He was moving out to California to begin a new class in Los Angeles.

One morning Milton called me in for a meeting. He had approved my position in class after he allowed me to do a scene. I loved the class and I behaved — well, to a point. I was still outspoken. Secretly I was told he loved my passion and found me challenging, as most actors were afraid of him. It was naturally common for me to speak up and give an alternative opinion, like when he announced to the class that on the gate at Delos was an ancient saying, "Know thyself."

And I blurted out, "And nothing in excess."

He always wanted to have the last word, and ignored me.

"But, Milton, how do you know who you are if you don't know your excesses?" I said.

He turned himself around in his swivel chair with cigar in hand and retorted, "Would you like to teach the class?"

The class had a laugh and again I shut up.

With all that in mind, I went to the meeting wondering what all this was about. I sat in his office while he just stared through me. It was always his way of intimidating. I just stared back, like it was natural. Then the silence was broken with a question that floored me.

"How would you like to come out to California and be my assistant?"

For once I was stuck for words. And so I replied, "No, thanks."

Now he was stunned. "Do you realize that I was the assistant to Elia Kazan, one of the most honored and influential directors on Broadway and in Hollywood history, and now you'll be mine? Do you know what that means?"

"I know, but I don't like you," I responded.

"You don't like me?" he said, aghast.

Holding my ground, I said, "No, I don't."

"I'll pay you to leave the fashion world and help set you up in L.A. You're an actor and you show great promise."

That was the first time I had ever heard him say that, and it hit a core. I was finally on my way as Dykshoorn had predicted, so I decided to follow the path and relented.

He was pleased, but this change in direction made me apprehensive. I went to see Meledandri, who had asked me to open up a new shop in Georgetown, Washington, D.C., and run the business. When I told him of my decision to move to Los Angeles to pursue my acting career, he was flabbergasted.

"Acting? I am giving you a great opportunity and you tell me acting?" He was very upset and broke a coat hanger.

I told him how much I appreciated all that he had taught me but now I finally found where my heart lies. It was emotional for both of us. We hugged and l left the premises for the last time. Years later while running in Central Park in New York, Roland Meledandri died of a heart attack at age fifty-one. What a loss — a talent not fully realized, but another great teacher for me along the path.

I spent many years as Milton's assistant, and in all those years we never had an argument. I loved him very much for he became the mentor that I had been searching for since my youth. We were always on the same page, and the classes were an enormous success.

One evening he invited Gloria Swanson of *Sunset Boulevard* fame to come to the class to inspire his students. Everyone was excited to meet this mythical star. The stage curtains were closed while I went outside to await the arrival of her limousine. When she exited the car a very slight and frail woman appeared.

"Hullo, darling, could you be a gentleman and carry me in as my legs are not what they used to be?"

"Well, of course," I said.

So I lifted the star into my arms and carried her into the theatre. I placed Miss Swanson in a chair while the curtain was still drawn. When the curtain opened she drew a standing ovation. Everyone was stagestruck.

She spoke for an hour, sharing her great life with students who were just in their beginnings. As she stood to leave, there was enormous applause and the curtain closed. I picked her up again and carried her to the car. No one had witnessed her fragility. She kissed me on both cheeks and disappeared like an illusion, befitting her star quality.

Many more famous stars — including Peter Finch, Cary Grant, John Cassavetes and his wife Gena Rowlands — came through the doors at Katselas' class, leaving imprints on our minds of what is possible when that kind of success happens to you. It was a gift to share it all with Katselas.

And together Milton and I experienced the unforgettable tragedy that befell actor Sal Mineo. Milton was directing Sal and Keir Dullea in *P.S. Your Cat Is Dead,* a new play by James Kirkwood premiering at the Westwood Playhouse in Los Angeles. It was February 12, 1976.

The great thing about assisting Milton with these pros was that the drama of life was always left on the stage. Sal had the reputation of living a shadowed life at night while his days were lightness and health-centric. Keir was a more reserved actor, keeping his personal life away from the rehearsals. His greatest fame was Kubrick's *2001: A Space Odyssey*.

Mineo was an iconic star, nominated twice for an Oscar. *Rebel Without a Cause* with Natalie Wood and James Dean and *Giant* with Dean resonated with my growing up in Australia. And here he was before me, just a normal actor except I'm sure most people rarely regard actors as "normal." To me he was an actor looking for a comeback, navigating his way through the maze of Hollywood.

On that February afternoon Milton — who always enjoyed fine cuisine — was telling the actors how much he loved my Greek lemon soup. Sal asked if it was possible for me to prepare some as an early dinner while they rehearsed. Little did I realize that my Greek lemon soup would be the last meal of Sal Mineo's life. I went to the store to shop for the ingredients along with an organic hen — Sal's request. Two hours later I served the frothy soup with toasted bread. It was a great success and to this day I remember the sated smiles.

After the rehearsals broke, I cleaned the dishes, and as I was wrapping up, Sal came to the kitchen and thanked me for making his day. A big hug later, he left with the promises of tomorrow. I exited with Milt to attend the classes he taught at the Beverly Hills Playhouse. Milton thrived on Tuesdays and Thursdays when conducting his scene study classes. Upon arriving home that night, I turned on the television and Sal Mineo's face filled the screen. The man who hugged me with gratitude earlier that evening was dead. Mineo was parking his car when out of the dark his murderer took a knife and stabbed him in the heart. As his assailant ran off, Sal's lovely heart burst.

The next day we all sat in shock as the police questioned us. They revealed some of the details of the murder and questioned us about Mineo's lover. The actor had never discussed his relationship with any of us, so we were little help to the authorities. After they left, a lone figure appeared at the theatre's entrance. He seemed to have been up all night, his face revealing the pain through the searing tears that raced down his face. Milton reached out to him and told him to see a doctor and to call the police. He didn't have much to say except in a daze he quietly uttered, "Thank you, thank you." He left as mysteriously as he had arrived.

For two years the police searched in vain for clues to the killer's identity, but nothing turned up. What feels particularly enigmatic about this tragedy are the deaths of his other *Rebel* castmates, Natalie Wood and James Dean. They too died tragically. They all died young.

We continued with the play and I truly understood what they meant by the cliché "the show must go on." Milton was a great leader and knew how to keep his team together. The show was a great success and played all over the United States.

Years later, out of the blue, the Michigan authorities reported that while Lionel

Williams was serving a sentence for writing bad checks, he bragged to fellow inmates that he had killed Sal Mineo. It was his wife who finally settled the story, telling the police that her husband had come home the night of the murder drenched in blood. He was eventually convicted and given a sentence of life in prison.

Our dear friend Sal died not because of some dark energy that he was associated with but by being an innocent, happily heading home after having rewarded us with his presence and his work. So at times like this, don't tell me any of us have the answers to life. It's a difficult process not always understood.

The Professional Life

Days of Our Lives was thought by many to be my first breakthrough, but I maintain it was the play *Jockeys*, directed by Milton Katselas and produced by Jule Styne in New York, that began it all.

That led to my first starring role in *Slow Dancing in the Big City*, directed by John Avildsen, an Oscar winner for *Rocky*. He was a dream to work with because he maintained a quiet demeanor on set. His direction was the same, privately and without criticism. And I loved the way he danced.

I returned to L.A. and continued to study with Milton while performing in *Play With Fire* produced by Telly Savalas at the Geffen Playhouse. I starred alongside Carrie Snodgress and Victor Buono in the role of a monk.

The play received terrific reviews, and a casting director from the Ahmanson Theatre contacted me to audition for *A Man for all Seasons* starring Charlton Heston and Vanessa Redgrave. After three callbacks with director Jack O'Brien I met with Heston, who had final approval. I have always looked upon Heston as a hero since watching him in one of my favorite films of all time, *Ben-Hur*. He was such a gentleman and so supportive when we read together.

He commented how much he appreciated the simplicity in my approach to the role of Richard Rich. It looked like I had the part, when my agent got a call that a Broadway actor coveted the same role. I was offered the part of the understudy. I refused, and they threatened that if I did not take the understudy role I would never work at the Ahmanson. And that threat came true. I never did, and that person died of a heart attack soon after while sitting on a toilet. Angry and disappointed as I was, life does take care of things on its own.

Jockeys in New York with Chick Vennera and Simone Griffeth. (Author's Collection)

John Avildsen directing Anne Ditchburn and myself. (Author's Collection)

With the visual wizard Ken Russell in Chihuahua. (Author's Collection)

With Charles White-Eagle and William Hurt. (Author's Collection)

At about the same time, I was called to audition at Paramount Studios for Ken Russell's *Altered States*, written by the wonderful Paddy Chayefsky and starring William Hurt. It was a successful audition and Russell chose me for the part of Echeverria, a botanist living in Mexico. It was a great script to be shot on the Warner Bros. lot and in Chihuahua, Mexico. I was beside myself having the opportunity of working with such talents. Unfortunately it would turn out to be one of the worst experiences of my life.

On the first day of shooting with Blair Brown, Bob Balaban and Charles Haid, the actors decided to be drunk as the script required, only they really were drinking since 7 a.m. I decided to be the only one sober and Russell agreed.

Everything was going well when Paddy Chayefsky came over to me and whispered in my ear, "I don't know where they found you, but you are exactly what I wrote." I smiled and thanked him. Apparently Russell thought he was giving me direction. Then there was an explosion on the set when the director called the writer a "cunt" and told him to "leave his set immediately."

Paddy replied, "You're the cunt," and the war of harsh words and emotion escalated until Russell demanded he leave the set or else he would walk. The executive producer tried to intervene but the chaos continued. Chayefsky eventually left the set and took his name off as writer of the film. What a beginning. As the Greek saying goes, "If it stinks in the beginning it smells in the end."

Along the way some of the comments passed on to me was that Russell enjoyed the work exchange between us. He had attacked almost everyone, including Blair Brown. After shooting my first scene on a Mexico mountaintop with William Hurt, Russell seemed happy with the progress. While walking along a path he told me how happy he was that I didn't sound like an Australian with that "hideous" accent. I told him how much I loved his last film, *Women in Love*, which won him an Oscar nomination. To this day it is still one of my favorite films.

It was a far from peaceful set. Russell began drinking his white wine during work to the point where it got excessive. There was a sequence where two very tall trees over a hundred years old were in the way of his shot. He demanded they be cut down. When the Mexican crew did as they were told he said the shot still didn't work. He began to be hated on the set and this "madman" (as he was now being called) was losing control. Due to his fair English skin and too much wine his face was blistering, so I suggested some vitamin E to keep the swelling down. It helped and he was grateful.

It was an amazing landscape with the indigenous Indians filling in the background. A week later we were on the final scene exiting the tribal area when Ken Russell began cutting things. The scene called for an argument with Hurt's character and my character's response to the hallucinogens that he had taken to expand his mind. I had a full-page monologue that expressed my views on his experience. Now it was being cut in half by Russell. When I commented that we had all signed a document written by Chayefsky that no dialogue was to be changed without his approval, he just exploded.

"I'm the director here, so just *fucking* do it."

I was stunned and confused. I now lost the meaning of the condensed scene.

The crew set up the shoot in a wide area the size of a football field. The camera and Russell were a distance away as they drove toward us, zooming in on our conversation. I couldn't remember the lines and I kept struggling with the interpretation. Take after take took place until Russell, who was absolutely furious, came at me with an empty wine bottle.

Screaming his lungs out so all could hear, the director walked toward me with such hate in his voice. "Why didn't you tell me you were a fucking amateur?"

William Hurt did not support me, moving away when he saw Russell threateningly coming toward me.

As he raised his empty wine bottle I stood my ground and thought *Don't you fucking dare*. I was ready to punch that bloated face if he did.

He backed off and quietly said, "Let's try again."

Suddenly I slipped into survival mode and, filled with raw emotion, William and I did five perfect takes. When it was over I stole straight to my trailer and sobbed my eyes out. I had never been so humiliated. During that last night, I was having dinner with Hurt and the crew when Russell walked in with two bottles of Dom Perignon, applauding our work. He sat down with us, oblivious to the trust he had annihilated.

The movie was a success and today is considered a classic. Years later while doing *Mission: Impossible* in Australia, I was asked to host the national daytime talk show with Ken Russell as my first guest. He was directing the opera *Madame Butterfly* in Melbourne. I told my producer at Channel Nine about my experience, and his advice was: "If he causes any disruption, just cut him off by saying 'And now a word from our sponsor.'"

Oh my, a little power over Ken sounded delicious.

Ken appeared via satellite and was jovial, and reminded me what a "wonderful experience we had making the film." That Hurt and I were "great actors with a job well done."

I was stunned by his niceness, and for the first time since that film a healing took place. Ah, well, drama was his game and I played it with him. He died in November of 2011 of Alzheimer's.

Dame Edna presented in Godowni's Court. (Author's Collection)

The Shining Dame

One of the greatest and most memorable experiences I've had in the industry was with Dame Edna, whom I consider to be one of the most hilarious human beings of the 20th century. His real name is Barry Humphries, but with costume, a wig and a high-pitched voice he morphs into a suburban housewife and international celebrity. A great star in England and an Australian treasure, his wicked humor consistently had people laughing in the aisles.

I met Barry in the late '80s in a restaurant in Sydney. He made a great entrance with a black cape and hat and then proceeded to assess me. They were looking for an Australian actor to play Dame Edna's love interest in *Les Patterson Saves the World*, directed by George Miller. I passed the test and we hit it off immediately. I played Colonel Godowni, an Arab leader with charm who became smitten with the Dame covering as a CIA spy.

It was another chance to go home and secure my family's belief that Dykshoorn was right. My parents embraced me especially for the fact that I was working with an Australian icon. After all, they always wanted to see their children reach greater heights than they had.

I loved the director George Miller. He was a regular Aussie with a terrific sense of humor. While rehearsing a scene and trying to find my footing, George blurted out, "Lovely performance, Thaao, just take three weeks out of it, will you?" He could have said "Too bloody slow, Thaao," but instead he did it without ridiculing me. That was the difference in bringing the best out of an actor without having to be a tyrant.

In one of the interviews I did with Dame Edna, the reporter asked, "I hear this is a great love story. Why do you think Dame Edna fell in love with the Colonel?"

"It was the uniform," Edna responded happily.

I then replied, "Well, I think it was the day when she walked into my room with those Joan Crawford shoulders and when I dropped my drawers she fainted."

Dame Edna was not amused. You see, she was a bit of a puritan and that joke was below the belt.

We worked together for two months creating a love story that had us laughing hysterically between takes. There was such a difference when Barry was his normal self. He was much more serious, and when in character as Edna another light shined through.

He kept his alter ego separate, never allowing the illusion to be broken. One day I was sitting in his trailer having a chat between takes when the assistant director came by with his camera and tried to take a photo as Edna was shaving. No longer in character, he used his normal voice when he said, "Don't you fucking dare!"

It was always important for him to never smash that myth with his public. He had to be protective of that and always on guard. I traveled with him for three weeks all over Australia doing publicity, and he opened his door to me. One day he told me that he and his wife Diane wanted to renew their vows, and would I be his best man? I was very touched by the gesture and gratefully complied. We kept in touch for many years after that, and I will still say today there has never been a funnier, more gracious man than Barry Humphries — he lit up my life.

On set in *Les Patterson Saves the World*. (Author's Collection)

Metaphysics, Katherine and Diane

When I arrived in Los Angeles I began my studies of metaphysics. I learned to meditate, and that helped eradicate some of the demons I had carried since childhood — getting rid of the shadows that frightened me, and to better understand and place light on fears.

My teacher was Katherine Hayward — an inspiring woman from England who understood my insights and limitations. When I first entered her house she immediately read my aura. "How dare you come here with the mind you have and the trash you associate with?"

I was stunned and did not return for another six months.

When I returned she said with a knowing smile, "Well, now you're ready to listen."

I continued to study with her for the next twelve years. She was extraordinarily perceptive. The knowledge I gathered from her still lights my way. When she died I felt the teacher had released her student to continue and live on by incorporating her work.

During the late '70s, I met another student on the path, actress Diane Ladd. We became great friends, and her knowledge of metaphysics was powerful. We embraced much on the subject and she helped me understand the feminine quality of life. A tremendous talent, Diane and I shared the screen when I played a mysterious character in the movie *The Lookalike*, directed by the wonderful Gary Nelson.

When Diane was nominated for an Oscar in 1990 for *Wild at Heart*, she asked me to escort her to the ceremony. What a thrill that was for a Sydney boy to attend his first Oscar ceremony. Diane had been nominated for an Oscar three times but never won. But she certainly won many other awards.

I always felt that by weaving spiritual understandings into her characters, Diane delved into other dimensions. It was as if the knowledge came through her, not from her. Her ego never interfered. I learned so much from Diane, on and off screen.

Shirley, Barbra and Bella

One afternoon I stopped by a good friend's home to deliver a Greek dessert for her to serve at a special brunch she was hosting. As I made my way into the kitchen I overheard Barbra Streisand, Shirley MacLaine, Bella Abzug and my friend, artist Ann Farrell, discussing an affair one of them was having with Prime Minister Pierre Trudeau of Canada. Standing quietly in the kitchen so as not to intrude, my ears perked up when his assets and passion became the subject of discussion. One of them said, "When you're finished with him, can I call him?" Since the conversation was heading to awkward territory, I made some noise to alert them to my presence. The conversation stopped abruptly and Annie came out to see who was there. "I'd ask you in, Thaao, but the conversation is very personal." "No kidding," I replied. As I was leaving I heard one of them ask, "Who was that?" "My Greek lover," she said. I heard someone say "Bring him back" as I walked out the door without looking back.

Three days later I was asked to have a read-through of the miniseries *Out on a Limb*, based on Shirley MacLaine's successful memoir. At the roundtable were MacLaine and the actor Tom Hulce along with producers and the writers. I was reading the part of her lover, a politician from Australia. The role would be played by Charles Dance in the television production. It was a true story that enveloped Shirley's spiritual saga in Machu Picchu, Peru.

Shirley had great energy and a powerful and determined gait. Everyone was introduced and Shirley quickly sat in front of me, eyes direct, legs apart and said, "Start." I was more amused than intimidated by the behavior. But I loved how fear

With Diane Ladd at the Oscars. (Author's Collection)

somehow didn't reside in her mind. I was facing a champion and she demanded that in return. Back and forward the dialogue went. Hulce was terrific as her adventurous guide, and I played the love aspect as convincingly as possible. Halfway through she asked for a break and without a word poured a cup of coffee. After a few minutes of silence she spoke and commented on my interpretation of her politician. "Thaao brought a sensitivity to the part that was not in the script, and I liked it a lot." She came up to me and gave me a great embrace. "Thanks for bringing that to the table," she said. And with that she smiled for the first time.

We continued through the rest of the day with great success. At the end of it Shirley mentioned a four-day seminar she was holding in Los Angeles and invited me to attend. It was through this experience that metaphysics returned to my playground, with new voices waiting to be heard. In a hotel near Los Angeles International Airport, four hundred people gathered and meditated as the host elevated our spirit through music and words that helped sing out the potential and eventual recognition of self.

Shirley told us great stories of how she went through her own adventures, overcoming the obstacles and managing and moving through each experience. That kept sharpening the tools she brought in, while enhancing her work as an actor by being in the present. I thought it a great event and an addition to the life experiences I would carry with me.

Omar

Omar Sharif was one of my favorite actors ever since I first saw him in the classic *Lawrence of Arabia*. So, when director Gary Nelson asked me to work with him again in the miniseries *Memories of Midnight* with Sharif and Jane Seymour, I did not hesitate. It was being shot mainly in Yugoslavia and Greece. The story was loosely based on the rivalry between Greek shipping magnates Aristotle Onassis and Stavros Niarchos.

On the first day in the makeup trailer in Zagreb, Omar sat next to me, and when we were introduced he simply responded with a nod. Appearing on the set, which was the actual house of ex-President Tito, Sharif made his majestic entrance and announced to me, "When I knock you down and you go flying over this 18th-century table, please don't break it."

"Oh, Mr. Sharif, if I let you knock me down in our first scene together we will have nowhere to go for the rest of the story. After all, I am your nemesis," I responded.

Suddenly the ice was broken and he embraced me with open arms, shouting out to the director, "I love this actor!"

With the wonderful Omar Sharif. (Author's Collection)

Now he looked upon me as a trusted thespian and whispered, "Do you like champagne and caviar?"

Surprised with his sudden behavior shift, I quickly replied yes.

"Good — after we break for lunch, come to my trailer and we will celebrate."

What a great beginning.

During lunch, Omar and I sat in his trailer like old friends, entertaining each other with wonderful stories complemented by delicacies befitting our appreciative tastes. He told me that I reminded him of his son but "the idiot married a hooker."

I asked him about *Lawrence of Arabia*, and he loved telling me the tales that Peter

O'Toole and he had experienced in their drunken stupor in Aqaba, Jordan. Because of the long shoot and the boredom in the extensive stretches of the desert landscape, they would get so intoxicated that they had to be tied to the camels so they wouldn't fall off. At one point, Omar said, the camel wouldn't stop and he ended upside down in the ocean and almost drowned.

That lunch lasted three hours, and every day we worked together the great stories continued. Except for one day when Omar had to go back to Paris and finish shooting another film; he returned exhausted. It was a big scene at an auction and our rivalry as the characters was heightened during a bidding war. He couldn't remember his lines and he kept flubbing. The director, knowing that Omar and I had developed a close relationship, took a break and asked me to take our star behind the curtain and have a talk. I did and in private Omar had a breakdown and cried on my shoulder. I will never forget that moment when he trusted me with his emotions. Vulnerable as he was, we went back and shot the scene with his professionalism intact. He never faulted again except when he told an actress at dinner that she wasn't very good at her craft, and the poor thing stormed off. He was a man who had worked with many great stars and made many classic films. His expectations were high.

When I said goodbye to Omar, a great sadness washed over me — and that was unusual. As an actor, you do the job you are hired for and then part ways, but not this time. He left me with such poignant memories. When I look back they had become part of me; they sharpened my being and sense of perspective. He invited me to visit him in Paris. I never did take him up on his offer and that I regret.

Impossible

I was able to go home again to Australia and shoot the series *Mission: Impossible* — and this time my father was really beaming. When I entered my father's house and felt his rare emotion with a warm embrace, it was magical. It healed all those years of doubts — his and mine — and proved that making your own decisions at a young age can lead to success.

I loved working with the team of *Mission: Impossible*. Peter Graves was always the pro, and the rest of the cast — Tony Hamilton, Phil Morris and the lovely and talented Jane Badler — all loved him too. We all got along and everything was going well until one day I was called to the producer's office, where I was delicately advised to cut my eyelashes. I told them that my mother calls them her "Vroutsoutses" — her "little brushes" — and she would be very upset if they were cut.

I was given the pilot to watch and was told I could make up my own mind about my lashes. After viewing it, I said no. I found nothing disturbing about the eyelashes, and besides, that's who I was. They were accepting and I continued playing my multifaceted character without any more comments on my little "brushes."

What I loved most about *Mission* were the disguises that allowed my character to infiltrate enemy territory while interacting with the rest of the team in those intrigue-filled episodes. I had to rise especially early on disguise days to have a mask fit to my face. It would become claustrophobic when I had to wait around for hours. Thanks to meditation I was able to control it some of the time. The masks would then have to be carefully removed because of the expense. It was part of the job and everyone did their part to bring a seamless ensemble to the screen. We were a great team.

Peter Graves, always the gentleman, passed in 2010 of a heart attack — he was a great guy from the old school. Tony Hamilton died tragically at forty-two of AIDS-related pneumonia. He had been adopted at two years of age from England by an elderly couple and brought to live in Australia, but he always felt like he didn't belong. He did some crazy things that put him in hot water with the studio. He lived his many lives to the fullest and paid for that decadence. But I felt that even though he appeared ruthless, he was like a little boy that never felt loved.

With Phil Morris, Peter Graves, Jane Badler and Antony Hamilton. (Author's Collection)

Endings

After *Mission* ended I returned to the U.S. to see my mentor Milton Katselas. He was semi-retired now and only taught the Master Class on Saturdays. He'd become a diabetic and lost three of his toes. His great pastime was basketball, but when he lost his footing something had died within him.

One early morning we were sitting in his courtyard in West Hollywood discussing our lives. He had a great career in the theatre and directed some of the country's top stars, but when he was fired by Elizabeth Taylor and Richard Burton in *Private Lives* something in him had shut down. He always loved his actors but some could never take his directness. He was a Scientologist and even by them he felt betrayed.

I asked about his greatest disappointment. After much thought he simply replied, "People." I thought at that moment he was thinking about those he brought closer to him and that trust was paid with betrayal.

And yet when a student had a "win" in this difficult business he was overjoyed as it reflected on him and his teachings.

Milton Katselas was the greatest influence of my life and the ultimate teacher in every way as my guide and my friend. He helped me look at my insecurities like they were my children, to nurture them and create from them. He taught me not to be afraid of my own personal expression. If we are fortunate, such people come just once this way in our lives. I was truly blessed.

I miss him dearly. He passed in 2008 at the age of seventy-seven not long after that special early morning talk. He took an excess of potassium and fell into a coma.

If he had asked me the same question, I would have answered the same way. "People."

"We are the choices we make," I wanted to tell him, but I never wanted to presume that I knew more than my teacher — that I had an insight into the pain he never overcame. We never did say goodbye.

Milton Katselas. (courtesy Mark Gantt)

Days of Our Lives informal cast portrait. (Author's Collection)

II. DODGING BULLETS

It was the late winter of 2009 when Ken Corday, executive producer of *Days of Our Lives*, left a message on my service. I was on a spiritual mission in Cuba visiting churches in pursuit of experiencing "faith" in a communist country.

Most churches in Havana are Roman Catholic, filled with statues of martyrs casting sadness rather than offering revelation. I was fascinated mostly by the Santería religion whose roots stemmed from Nigeria and were transported to the Caribbean by the Lucumi people in the late 18th century. I had also heard that the ancient priests of Egypt used the power of these rituals for imparting knowledge to the Pharaohs.

The day I received the message from Ken I had a session with a Babalao, a priest of the Santería religion based on the worship of nature. I had been transported by car to the outskirts of Havana where the police, secret or in uniform, were always visible, sometimes stopping or following us by car. I was on another adventure in unknown territory and was looking forward to this new experience.

In a private backyard surrounded by an abundance of plants, all sacred to the rituals, I was stripped and cleansed with herbs in front of a "shrine of worship" filled with deities. This was a sacred space where the initiate is "born again." I became instantly aroused simply standing there in front of these sacred icons. I was embarrassed. But the Babalao shrugged it off. "It's about power," he said, putting up his fist, "your power."

A chicken was sacrificed as part of the closing ceremony. It screeched loudly in disapproval and was rubbed all over my body. And then silence. I had to face away from the deities when the animal made its transition.

At the last stage of the ceremony I was instructed to turn around as the priest dropped three open coconuts at my feet. How the coconuts fell would reveal the final outcome of this secret ceremony. All three turned up white and were touching one another.

The priest smiled and said, "It is a good omen when the spirits have sent you kisses."

With penetrating eyes he quietly told me that he had removed a knife from my back, placed there by a dark spirit. "That's why the chicken was sacrificed. It absorbed the negative energy from you and died. It's what you have been carrying for at least a year."

My mind rattled. Who placed this "knife"? Something did seem amiss that morning. And I was cloaked in a feeling that a confrontation was imminent. The imagery didn't help. Perhaps that's why I had been drawn to the Santería and not Catholicism for answers. It was a different solution. One that gave me guidance from outside sources, while the other gives guidance from within.

The High Priestess of Havana. (Author's Collection)

After this intense day I needed to return to the hotel and call my home in Los Angeles. Our cell phones weren't functional in Cuba. I arrived at the hotel two hours later, having enjoyed the wonderful but deteriorating architecture along the way. I loved watching that decadence of fallen beauty, manifested by Cuba's history of struggle. I began thinking about my experience of being cleansed when the euphoria set in.

The message from Ken Corday back in Los Angeles instantly killed the euphoria. I needed to call "right away" and that could only mean one thing: another tragic death for my character Tony DiMera on *Days of our Lives*.

As I waited on the phone I filled with dread. Producers rarely call to give you good news. The silence was broken when Ken came to the phone. My intuition was correct.

"We have decided to kill the character off again as this team of writers and producer are going in a different direction. You have sixteen more episodes and I'm sorry."

In other words, the death of my character was a sorry plot twist for someone in that group who was not feeling inspired. I knew it was the new executive producer who came to the show a few months back. I was reminded of the time I was in the hall at NBC talking to the stage manager when an unfamiliar man walked down the hall toward me. I thought, *If this is an actor he should play Iago* — a character in *Othello* who just oozed a mastery of sinister deception.

He reached out his hand and introduced himself. "Hello, Thaao, I'm your new executive producer." We both smiled, but from his tone and manner I knew at that moment I was dead. My instincts were right.

It had not been a great time on the set recently as many of the actors and crew were experiencing cuts in their salaries, and the exits were rampant.

"There will be at least six actors killed off in the next few months" was the word in the shadowed halls.

The workload was becoming intense as well — two or three shows shot a day was the norm. The pressure was exhausting and everyone wondered who was leaving next.

The atmosphere was tense. But everyone remained on their toes and our work was diligent. Sadly, it was no longer the joyous place I had remembered for so many years, driving through those gates in Burbank when the studio was at its peak.

I first came to the attention of *Days of Our Lives* producers after a successful run on *General Hospital*. My *General Hospital* character was Victor Cassadine. I was hired by Gloria Monty to be part of the aristocratic and entertaining Cassadine dynasty, along with John Colicos and Andre Landzaat. *General Hospital* was experiencing unprecedented daytime success and the Luke/Laura/Cassadine storyline made soap opera history. "Luke and Laura" were on the cover of *Newsweek* magazine, christening

General Hospital "TV's Hottest Show." Not daytime television. Television, period. Elizabeth Taylor was such a big fan she didn't miss one single episode of the goings-on in Port Charles. A character was eventually written just for her. When I was hired for the role I had no idea of its popularity.

I had come off the success of *Altered States*, and a SAG strike was looming. Work started to shut down and the only acting gigs available were in daytime, under the jurisdiction of AFTRA. The strike became the longest in the Guild's history. For nine months actors struggled. Me included. Nearly broke, I could not continue to wait for movie opportunities, so I took the first available job and tested for *General Hospital*. I secured the part of a glamorous villain and became one of the first British-sounding characters to be cast in an American soap opera. Tastes were changing and producer Gloria Monty was a visionary. She was small in frame but tough as nails. Thirty actors were selected for that big summer storyline. If you were trying to get on her best side by complimenting her too much, she would quickly dismiss you. The best way to reach her tight heart was to bring your professionalism to the set, know your lines and exit. She had no time for small talk. When Gloria was on set I always ignored her by having my head stuck in a book. This made her curious, and the more I played that game the more she would approach me and ask how I was doing. I learned early on not to feed the power of those who already had it.

Toward the end of the run one of the lead actors, machine gun in hand, grabbed me by the chest while overemphasizing his machismo during a scene, screaming out, "Shut up, Victor." Pulling on my hairy chest in a way over-the-top fury didn't quite make sense and it did not resonate well with the producer. I shouted in pain when Gloria came stomping out. With a pencil in hand she very intensely said to the nervous actor who tried to interrupt, "No, no, why do you need to grab him like that when you already have the upper hand with the gun? You see this pencil, all I have to do is break it next to your name in the next script and you're dead." It was a woman in power at her best. Men were intimidated because she held all the cards.

The show was so huge that college students gathered in lounges and dorm rooms to watch *General Hospital* five days a week. Bars would change channels to *General Hospital* and offer pizza and beer specials. For the first time in my life I experienced what it was like to be part of a cult classic. *General Hospital* mania was everywhere. Just before our contracts were up, some of the actors hired only for the summer storyline were called into Gloria's office for her condolences and thanks for a summer that made television history. My "brother" Andre and I shared a dressing room, and he was the first one summoned by Gloria. He returned dejected and with tears rolling down his face. "Can you believe that bitch? I'm going to die on the show next week and when I said, 'But what about my fans?' she said, 'Oh, fuck your fans.' Can you believe it? Well, good luck, you're next."

As I entered her sanctuary, Gloria stood up to shake my hand. I was stunned when she asked me to sit down. "How does it feel to be the only one out of thirty actors to survive this summer storyline? We want you back and I must say, darling, it is my pleasure to have you on my show. We'll bring you back after you have spent some time in prison for your crimes. The public will forgive you and a great love story will bloom." She smiled as I said thank you for the great privilege. When I went back to my dressing room, right away Andre wanted to know when I was dying. After I gave him the news all he could say was, "What did I do wrong?"

Elizabeth Taylor joined the show as my sister-in-law as I was being led to prison. We never worked together, but I had the opportunity to meet her at a *General Hospital* party. I approached her table and on one knee introduced myself. What a gorgeous broad. I had fifteen minutes with her, and even today I cannot remember any of the conversation because for the first time in my life I was starstruck. Those violet eyes were so seductive that when I got up, I kissed her hand and left in a daze. When the other actors asked me what we talked about, I smiled gleefully and honestly replied, "I have no idea."

At the time, I didn't return to Port Charles because the head writer, Pat Falken Smith, left the show and requested that I go with her to *Days of Our Lives*. When I did make the move to *Days*, Gloria Monty was not happy. One of the trade papers the next week carried the headline "The One That Got Away." And I did. (Decades later, in early 2014, they would eventually bring Victor back to Port Charles. Twitter was abuzz with news of my return to the daytime landscape and episodes are just starting to air as this book goes into production.)

After testing for the role of Tony DiMera on *Days*, I felt I was tested again by some of the more established actors who responded to the new actor on the block with indifference. Even the lovely MacDonald Carey was aloof. When I approached him one day at lunch he offered a harsh lesson on the life of an actor in daytime that I would never forget:

"I don't spend much time getting to know new actors on the show anymore because in the past when I had and they were killed off, it was a painful process to go through. Now I treat them with a slight curiosity, with no emotional investment."

As time passed and it became apparent I was there to stay, the attitudes toward me changed. They were a great group of pros that welcomed me into their family with a warm embrace. Learning pages and pages of dialogue every night was the biggest challenge, until a producer gave me the best insight to overcome this. "Don't look at how many pages there are, as you will get overwhelmed. Take one scene at a time, be in the present and that way you stay in control." It worked.

On weekends we did a lot of charity work, and one experience still resonates to this day. I had been requested to do a Q&A and autograph session appearance in the Midwest. Thousands of fans appeared for the event, and afterward I received a call from the local hospital. The mother of a young lady asked if it was possible for me to stop by the Cancer Center for Children on my way to the airport to meet her daughter, Rose. She had only three months to live, and the deeply caring mother said that surprising Rose would be a "dream come true." Apparently she was a big fan of the show and of my character in particular.

I asked the driver to stop by a florist to buy two dozen roses. The mother met me at the front desk of the hospital, truly elated that I had come. When I entered Rose's room she was overwhelmed. I presented her with the red roses and she cried and whispered, "Tony, Tony, Tony." Her knight in shining armor leaped out of the television set and like a fairy tale was holding her in his arms. For a brief moment in this girl's life I could feel some healing taking place when celebrity was used to make a difference. We sat together like old friends, and she mentioned how she loved the romance on the show and all of the unrequited love. She bravely spoke of her cancer and how limited her life had been. When I had to leave to catch my plane our embrace was long and emotional. I silently wondered why children are sent into this life only to discover disease and the struggle to survive, affecting all those surrounding them? Those answers never came.

Over the months her mother kept in touch and on occasion I spoke with Rose and kept up the illusion of "Tony," never smashing the myth. Rose survived beyond those three months initially predicted by the doctor's prognosis and continued to live another four years. It was when "Tony" mysteriously left the show (disappearing into a fog) that our Rose passed away. She held on that long. Through the fantasy she imagined, Rose lived her last years happier by knowing that her hero did exist and had acknowledged her with roses. Her mother said when Tony left it was time for her as well. It moved me to tears.

And now they were saying that NBC stood for "Nobody Cares." This was to be my sixth death. That sounds comical but we were living through the imagination of head writer "Riley the Maestro." Being killed off created a feeling of sadness within

Opposite Page: Cassadine Days. The night I met Elizabeth Taylor at a *General Hospital* benefit. (Author's Collection)

me, and in some instances, silent joy. It meant that my comfort zone was being challenged and I would be leaving the show for new horizons. No regrets, just being in tune with life's changes and trusting the process.

Meanwhile, back in Cuba I sat with this news and my stream of memories. I spent my remaining days in Havana with artists I had met along the way. The simplicity in the way they lived, surrounded by poverty, their passion and love flowing freely, revealed how indulgent I had become with the rewards life had given me. It reminded me of Saint Francis' teachings of being satisfied with little, like the birds, without being stuck with possessions.

I sat with these artists and together we drank an entire bottle of vodka while sharing tales of Castro's Cuba and life in Hollywood. I gave my host a watch as a gesture of thanks. His guests were amazed at my generosity, and I thought nothing of it. It was ultimately a betrayal of my ignorance that a simple gift of thanks would eventually cause tremendous havoc in an oppressed region. Police would soon be stopping him on the street. Given the quality of his newly acquired watch, they would accuse him of stealing and smash his wrist against the wall. He would let out a loud cry and they would arrest him. He was eventually discharged. All this commotion took place because he had been given a gift he himself could not afford.

That lack of freedom struck me hard, knowing their inability to afford anything because of low wages and the longing they had to escape their prison just to see how the rest of the world existed. I thanked them for their hospitality and I left with the promise of a return. When I was leaving, I noticed a painting hanging over the host's kitchen table. It was a large-sized canvas, light in color with a hollowed center. I asked him, the artist of the striking painting, what the work represented.

"It's my escape from Cuba," he replied.

Two years later he did just that. Now he is a respected artist in Miami.

I was returning home to California to face another challenge, but this time I was prepared. Filling myself up with another culture always gives me confidence and a clearer head on how to proceed. At that moment I laughed, thinking about a line from *A Man for All Seasons* — "Death comes to us all, my friends, yes, even for kings he comes."

Death can signify a major transition, and I had seen it through many times before. It was the "going through it" that was the obstacle course. Knowing that you were leaving the daytime world — again — while keeping up appearances was part of the norm.

Pondering possibilities and probabilities. (Author's Collection)

Over the years I saw how other actors reacted during their last days. When you are called up to a producer's office it usually signifies change. The door closes behind you and you face the expression of doom. Some become angry and others are relieved. The fact is that they are telling you that your services are no longer required. It can make an actor feel like they didn't make a difference.

It was now March 2009 and I was shooting my last two shows. I was in makeup when my producer, Ken Corday, walked in and wanted to know "when I was dying."

I told him on Monday and then took the opportunity to ask, "Why do I always have to die so violently? Can't I just disappear up the stairs?"

He smiled at me. "You'll be back."

"No, I won't," I replied abruptly. He stared back in anger and stormed off. It was the last time I saw or spoke to him, and I regretted that moment.

I have always liked Ken, as his employment was one of the main reasons I was able to afford my journeys. I found him to be generous and approachable with a great amount of spiritual awareness that we always shared. I brought him candles from Jerusalem along with the holy water from the Greek Orthodox Church in ancient Cairo, and he met these gifts from my travels with appreciation.

On one of my last days on the set I was lying down on my hospital bed, acting in serious condition after a horrific accident where a spike had pierced my chest. It would be another violent death. Deep down I felt resentful for having to go through this emotional and physical violence. It does have an effect.

I was glad I had gone to see the Babalao, as I now understood the image of the knife in my back. But I kept remembering the blessing from the spirits, and that helped me through it.

My character was unable to speak due to the accident, so my on-camera communication was executed by writing on a pad. I lay there in my hospital room where actors and crew were talking during a five-minute break. I looked up toward the studio ceiling and began to flash back to the last twenty-eight years at NBC where I was a member of a wonderful cast and played two terrific characters, the diabolical Count Antony and the evil twin Andre DiMera.

Dressing for my characters was one of my great joys on the set. I would fly once a year to Rome and buy my wardrobe, all paid for by NBC and Corday. It was a fantasy to walk into the Armani boutique on the Via dei Condotti and say, "I'll have that, that and that." It was an ego trip I took seriously.

The reward working for a popular soap opera was great abundance. But you had to earn it. They began shooting the hospital scene and I digressed into wonderful scenes of the past. Picturing Deidre Hall and Joe Mascolo play out their latest dilemmas, I tried to find the humor in it. I was getting emotional about them, as I loved them both. My very real emotions were captured on camera while my fellow actor James Scott was sharing his brotherly respect and regrets. When the scene was over and the tears from my digression were evident, James blurted out, "Even when you have no dialogue, you still steal the fucking scene." I laughed at the tragedy of it all. He joined in. I loved working with James because he was fun and always the professional. A half-brother whose onscreen conflicts with my character were bigger than life. Yet in real life there was never a misunderstanding between us. It was definitely a case of opportunity meets compatibility.

As the scenes continued I kept living through my history, remembering the joys and loves and the occasional murder. I thought about the many "deaths" of my characters.

It started with the head writer, James Reilly, who has since passed. When I first met him, a rare occurrence for any actor, James presented himself as a big jovial fellow, rather tall and overweight. He wore colorful bow ties and was cartoonesque and very funny, a character popping out of his own fairy tale.

Yet according to inside sources, actors did not exactly enthrall him. He was a puppeteer, and actors were to play according to his fantasies, and that was law. He painted a large canvas with an enormous penchant for storytelling. His way of creating began to be duplicated on other daytime soaps since our show's ratings had really moved up. It had been widely discussed that he changed the face of daytime by having this fresh imagination. The audience loved it and bought into it for a while, but as it got repetitive and cartoonish, the ratings fell. He was fired along with his team of writers.

During a break in filming, I joked with a fellow actor about the many times Reilley had killed me off. He heard that I had allegedly remarked that his scripts were shit. I argued that I had never said that. I was one of a few actors who performed what was written on the page and gave it my own spin. If the scene was difficult or repetitive, I found ways to make it work by trying to add to the writer's insight and thereby enjoying the challenge. It's what I was paid to do.

I always felt appreciated by the head writers until Reilly came along. I had been blinded in a previous storyline and, feeling creative, began to reveal the possibility that I was getting my sight back. I didn't know that six months down the road he was thinking the same thing. And now he was furious that I would anticipate his story ahead of time.

"Dead, dead, dead," was his response.

The "knife in my back" seed that was planted in Cuba tinkered with my notion of a safe workplace. I found myself distrusting some of my fellow actors and others who were working behind the scenes. It became clear to everyone that there was a snitch amongst us who would report to Reilly any scenarios that would be of interest to him.

Once I went to see a producer, and while calling out his name I noticed a reflection in a mirror by his office desk — there an actress was hidden against the other wall so as not to be seen. It was obvious I was walking into a clandestine meeting and there was the snitch. I never entered the room, as I didn't want to expose her. The producer asked me to come back later.

While returning to my dressing room I saw James Reilly walking down the stairs. My mind began to race, as I didn't want my presence known. Feeling like my villainous character Andre, I fantasized of pushing him down the stairs, but as luck would have it he would probably bounce. I had a chuckle and decided to let him disappear, as he would not have been happy if I had addressed him. Writers and producers avoid you when you're "dying." I realized I was holding a grudge for all the times he had been responsible for my being fired whilst every time he was dismissed I was asked back. And that happened three times.

He held true to his character: death to those who defy him. But to his credit he did write my characters in a Greek dramatic style, and that I enjoyed even though in one episode that meant wearing a top hat and entertaining an audience at the circus as a large bucket full of blood (made of a sugary substance) was about to fall on my head from forty-five feet above the ground. As they called "Action," a producer frantically called out "Stop!" Apparently he believed that the pressure of the liquid at that height falling on my head could cause the hat to cut my ears off.

When we started again, I took my hat off while announcing the highlights of the circus program. The "blood" poured down thunderously on my head, and as I stepped forward, I slipped on the sugary substance and fell on my ass. I got up laughing, covering my humiliation at the faux pas while the audience looked on in shock. Everyone was very helpful making sure I wasn't hurt. The only problem was that I had to stay in costume all day as the sticky material dried all over my hair and skin. Even my private parts suffered.

Then there was the time an escaped tiger, a real one, ominously stalked my character. He circled and then lunged for the attack. They put in a fake substitute while I screamed my lungs out, pretending the pain was unbearable. I died quickly then. Reilly was rid of me once again with yet another nasty scenario. The producers used to send him a bucket of ice cream and a case of champagne to feed his indulgences. He was clearly not a happy person.

In another storyline, a knife was thrown and lodged in my throat. The fans went into an uproar. By all accounts, I was dead. Two weeks later I returned on my yacht wearing a bandage. Reilly did have a sense of humor. I heard he loved watching the show while he made fun of the older actors whom he saw as "old cows." Apparently he cried out "Moooo" as he watched. He wanted them emptied from his canvas, and slowly but surely they were removed from the show.

When I returned to work after my parents passed, feeding the work helped delay those gutting emotions. I realized early on that the best place to mourn is through a creative outlet. But three months later I was summoned to the executive producer's office. As I entered, the door closed behind me with the touch of a button.

Two more grim faces had joined the party. I was given the news and was feeling pretty raw. "I understand," I told them. "But the next time you decide to kill an actor off could you do it after they have finished their scenes?" They apologized without emotion and I left, feeling confused with life. It's been documented that the most stressful thing to happen to a person is to lose a parent, child or job. I had a double whammy within months.

Someone in the booth confided in me when they heard the news.

He said, "Flies always snap at eagles."

I was told that their intention was to kill me three months earlier, but when my parents died they didn't want to appear insensitive — or so they said. At the end of my storyline they placed my character in a coffin, displayed for the family characters to emote their remorse. That was a tough ending, lying in that coffin. It's not a place many of us experience while we're still breathing.

When I returned home that night, I slid down on the kitchen floor and wept for hours at my parents' passing. It had finally hit me.

Those times of recognition don't come often, but when they do, the insight provided is immeasurable. Now I was in the front line facing my own mortality. I began to question my purpose in life, realizing that my dream was attached to my parents' approval. Now I had to create my own dream based on what I had become. The tears came with gale force, and when there were no more tears to cry I was completely drained. My heart, my soul, my spirit were all empty. Such a sad feeling, emptiness.

Writing became my outlet. What transpired are the stories that poured forth and are the makings of this book. It was not an easy transition because at the time the idea of acting seemed superfluous.

In circular fashion, Reilly was let go again and I was called back with a great return to the mythical city of Salem, and was met with a wonderful embrace by the new writers and producers. Ken Corday greeted me with open arms and I felt vindicated. But you never forget how you left.

Leann

Leann Hunley was the actor who made the biggest mark during my years on *Days*. I was always surprisingly calm in her presence. As an Australian, I come from a place where we call it as we see it. I became outspoken in my early days, and Leann helped me to see alternative viewpoints and ways to behave. I learned that not everyone sees your truth, and so I had to get used to "playing the game." As I matured, that turmoil within me began to dissolve.

We were a popular couple, full of romance and dance, and gave signature to the line "love in the afternoon." We never argued and that compatibility was evident on the television screen.

We broke boundaries, creating the first bathtub and shower scene in daytime television. That rubber ducky floating in the bathtub became part of a passionate love scene. The audiences loved it, especially when I told a public forum that during the scene Leann's right breast was beginning to expose itself above the bubbles as the water was running. While shooting I was trying to create more bubbles underneath the water to help cover the exposure. She was a good Christian girl who would have been mortified.

In the shower sequence she requested that I *do not* pull the zipper of her evening dress all the way down as it would expose the crack of her bum. So in my tuxedo I carried her into the shower and while the water was running I got so caught up in the love scene that I did the obvious. The zipper went slowly down to prohibitive territory. I was playfully slapped, deservedly so. To this day we are still great friends because of that foundation. She was a beauty, and still is today.

Some of the male actors were quite competitive with their machismo, wearing lifts and elevated heels to appear taller. One actor was always making fun about how much shorter I was than he. Well, boy did he get a surprise one afternoon when I entered his dressing room unannounced. Meaning, no lifts. He paraded about the room on his toes as if that were perfectly normal.

I had a good laugh. Some actors feel that if they are taller than you, it makes them more powerful, and their manhood is somehow elevated. But most of them were a great group of guys who loved the world they basked in. I felt the same. It was a great world of make-believe.

The diva roles were left to the women. We had a few who played that role fully, but Lauren Koslow, Kristian Alfonso, Deidre Hall and of course Leann were a joy. One day in the makeup and hair room I kidded with the women who spent a good deal of time there.

"My God, ladies, if you spent as much time on your acting as you did in makeup, could you imagine the performances?"

They got the humor and laughed, except for one who left in a huff. She was the least talented.

In the early '80s I worked with Brenda Benet, who was one of the most beautiful actresses I had ever known. Benet's son Christopher died tragically in 1981. She went into a severe depression but kept a brave face on set, never revealing that she was falling apart from within.

One day I brought in duck à l'orange that I prepared the night before. A few of my fellow actors gathered. Joe Mascolo contributed a bottle of champagne, while Philece Sampler (who played Renee, my love interest) and Brenda joined in for this rare occasion. We created a feast as a celebration of our lives. It was a lovely exchange that I will never forget because that night Brenda Benet went home, and while looking in the mirror, shot herself through the mouth.

She was only 36 years old.

It was indescribably shocking. Many tears were shed on set. The storyline had to be abruptly changed and the writers had their hands full. The raw emotions were filtered through our performances. Some of the female cast would break down in the middle of shooting. Life moved on but that tragic memory always lingers.

One of the most joyous scenes for me at *Days* happened when my character became an evil clown. I was playing two characters, one good and the other deadly. I thrived when for the first time I wore a clown's outfit. The shoes were huge and the makeup was brilliant. When I walked onto the set no one recognized me. I felt I could get away with murder. I created a voice from hell and began to terrorize the character of Sammy (Alison Sweeney) while she lay in her hospital bed.

She was fantastic in the role of the distressed heroine, and she hated clowns. When I heard that, I went to town. I brought her balloons and danced away around her hospital bed. I felt freer than I ever had before and unexpectedly threw myself onto a stool that glided me over to her at great speed. I climbed beside her and I began fondling her, as I knew she would be frightened and uncomfortable. I was hardly appealing.

Unpredictable and enjoying every moment as she squirmed, I reveled in the dark humor that came from God knows where. All I knew was that it was working and my acting partner's fear of the clown's maniacal behavior played off of it impressively. With my infamous words "All the world loves a clown" at the end of the first act, I applauded myself with my large red shoes while holding her hostage in my make-believe world.

In the final act of the terrorizing clown storyline I had to dress up as a nurse. After the last time they had put me in a dress and glamorized me, I ended up looking like an old hooker from Brazil. To make things worse, two male extras walked toward me and commented, "What an ugly transsexual."

(Courtesy American Media, Inc.)

That did it. Andre the Clown had to escape the Salem police, so he quickly got out of his clown costume and disguised himself as a nurse. I told wardrobe and the makeup department that I wanted to be unglamorous. With an old cardigan, '50s eyeglasses and low heels, and walking like a tired aunt, I felt more at ease as I was now controlling the joke. It was a lot of fun, and that performance earned me an Emmy nomination in the lead actor category. My brother George was in Los Angeles at the time, and when the news arrived early that morning I ran to the balcony and said, "George, I got a nomination." He looked up as I had disturbed his crossword puzzle and simply replied, "That's nice," and went back to his puzzle.

My brother has always been close and supportive of me, and I knew where his heart was. But when one producer said, "Is it in the supportive category?" I knew where *his* heart was. "No," I responded, "it's in the category you have not had in twenty years." The comments were mostly wonderful as it was always a supportive group. NBC was kind and sent their congratulations.

The night of the Emmys in 2009 was an incredible experience except for a producer who said "loser" after my loss. It was a bit jarring, but that was his kind of humor. I wished that my parents had been alive to see it. But my family was happy. At the after-party, our head writer approached me with her congratulations and told me about a new storyline she was developing for me in the fall about autistic children. I thanked her, not knowing that in the fall there would be no storyline in sight.

A few months later our executive producer, Ed Scott, was let go. I thought he was terrific in his position. He was full of passion, always cared about his actors and acknowledged performances that were worthy. He would charge onto the set like a bull in a china shop. What a difference his energy made. We all loved his style. He was a real straight shooter.

That's when Gary Tomlin came in to replace him. After months of no story I went up to his office for a meeting. I mentioned that I had received a nomination that year and wanted to know why there was no story.

He just looked at me and simply said, "It's not about talent, Thaao."

It shocked me, as I had not heard that in all my years as an actor. What kind of people are these that they would be thinking this way? I knew my time was up. I left his office and thought how I had studied my craft for so many years, believing from those who led before me that I could make a difference.

The truth that surfaced that day was a wake-up call. Ageism was rampant. A lifetime of learning and a world of experience did not resonate with them.

On set with Joe Mascolo, Brenda Benet and Philece Sampler the day before Brenda died. (Author's Collection)

Leann Hunley. (Photo: Jonathan Exley)

I thought back about those who had the same feelings as I, but they were disappearing. I was now on limited time.

As I was lying there for the final scene of the day, I came out of my conflicted thoughts when Joe Mascolo, who played my father on the show, came to give me an embrace. He had been saddened by news of my departure as we had played so many wonderful scenes together over the years.

He was a powerful being with a voice that bellowed like a mythical god. We shared great chemistry, especially when his authority was challenged. He was a perfect villain, which attested to his longevity on the show. There was no one like Joe, bigger than life. He loved classical music and opera. Once in a scene he had slapped my face so hard that I saw stars. I was stunned, but I played along as I turned slowly and wiped the slap off my face in defiance.

That's how unpredictable our scenes were. It was classic Greek tragedy, and we bonded with respect to that level of work. The DiMeras, as we were called, were a great foil to the heroes of the show. Let's face it, without good villains the challenges to the heroes of the show would not have been as effective.

I now had a new wife on the show named Kristen, who was played by Eileen Davidson. It was then that the dynamics changed for my character. She had betrayed me by having an affair with John Black, the show's macho hero. That storyline softened me, as I was at effect rather than at cause in this popular storyline. Eileen was terrific, and that year we both did some of our best work. She looked beautiful and was always present. It was at this time the blindness story set in and my anticipation to be creative set in motion my next death. It didn't help that this particular story was voted one of the worst by *Soap Opera Digest*, the publication otherwise known as the "bible of daytime." This probably irked him, and whatever the reason, writer James Reilly had the right to paint his canvas in the way he pictured it.

On my last day Gary Tomlin asked if I would like a cake for my farewell. I politely declined as I always regarded it as "the cake of death." After so many deaths I didn't need another reminder I was exiting. The cake of death typically happened during a break, and our executives would say their kind words in front of photographers with most of the actors and crew present. Then the cake of death would be cut and we would "celebrate" another demise.

Death is no stranger to daytime television. If a storyline got tired, a death could liven things up. If an actor wasn't renewing a contract, death was a viable option for a swift and dramatic exit. If an actor was aging, unruly or simply deemed unnecessary to the plot, dying brought drama and closure. On and off the camera — not to mention

On the lam, *Days of Our Lives*. (Author's Collection)

in the hearts of devoted fans — death was a fever pitch of emotion. As essential to the sands in the hourglass as love, marriage and birth.

I wanted to leave quietly and just go off into the next stage of my life without regrets. They were a great team doing complicated work in a business that was executed with breathtaking speed. I did dodge bullets staying alive in this very competitive game. You can't be loved by everybody, but with the training I had I can sincerely say I did my best.

Ken Corday made a difference in my life for the great education I got because of his embrace and the international appeal that brought us all onto the world stage.

When I finished my last scene, neither Gary Tomlin nor Ken Corday came to say goodbye. Gary had taken the day off. I thought I deserved better than that. Kindness is not expensive.

I initially resisted writing about my beginnings and soap opera career. I intended for this book to begin with my first trip to Egypt. That trip to one of Earth's most magical places changed everything for me. My success in acting allowed me to take the many journeys you'll read about in the pages that follow. Without my New York adventures, without my daytime television success and longevity, it's unlikely my travels would have been so extensive. Exploring the world the way I do presents all types of drama. All sorts of highs and all sorts of lows. Not unlike the journey of being a soap opera character. I was well prepared.

III. PLACES

A Discovery in Egypt 74	Dreaming of Casablanca 170
Climbing Mount Sinai 78	Christmas in Israel 184
Assisi 86	Lebanon 188
In the Footsteps of Moses 88	The Citadel 198
Transitions 94	The Way Out Is
Coming Full Circle 118	The Way Through 203
Hatshepsut and the	Alexandria: In Search of
Valley of the Kings 136	Alexander and Cavafy 209
The Great Escape 142	Ithaca 212
Discovering a Holy Site 157	Into Enemy Territory 216
Passage to Troy 161	Sunset at Giza 230
Ballooning Over the	The Elgin Marbles 234
Valley of the Kings 164	Kastellorizo 241

A Discovery in Egypt

MY FASCINATION WITH HISTORY, EGYPT IN PARTICULAR, BEGAN when I was twelve years old. It was then that my history class at Cleveland Boys High School was invited on an excursion to view an ancient mummy at the History Museum in Sydney, Australia. When we arrived, all in perfect order wearing our perfect uniforms, we stood in awe as a sarcophagus was opened and there before us lay a Pharaoh from Egypt's Golden Age. We stood there for fifteen minutes while our teacher described this wonder.

All I could absorb was that his hair was still there, and that at over 3,000 years old, it was still as brilliant a red as it ever was in life. His nails were long and dark, and his nose reminded me of Captain Hook. Most of my classmates reacted as though this were a scene out of a horror movie. As for me, I wanted to touch the sarcophagus. Any hands-on experience was completely prohibited, naturally. So we filed out as good students do, but my mind was still on the ancient mummy. I was fascinated and wanted more.

I waited until everyone left, then ran back while no one was watching. I climbed over the ropes and opened the lid of the sarcophagus. I knew that until I touched it I couldn't believe it was real. Against all odds, I carefully touched the hair, the nails and finally the nose. I felt a sense of exhilaration — a feeling that would be short-lived as my teacher, furious at my absence, ran in and promptly sent me to the headmaster for insubordination. As punishment, my hands were whipped four times with a bamboo cane. The pain was a small price to pay for such an experience. But what the hell, my life was just beginning.

Cheops' Pyramid. (Author's Collection)

One of my earliest dreams as a child was to visit Cheops' Pyramid in Egypt under a full moon. I came across a photograph of the Pyramid during my history studies and thought it surreal. So it was fitting that this would be the destination of my first journey to Egypt in the mid-'70s.

I arrived in Cairo, a world so alien from my surroundings in New York where I was living at the time. After winning a substantial amount of money playing blackjack at the hotel casino in Cairo, I impulsively hired a cab to drive me to Giza at 1 a.m. I was fortunate that it was such a clear night. Half an hour later, there in the distance I could see the silhouette of the great Wonder of Egypt. I couldn't wait to experience it at my feet.

Leaving the cab behind, I ran toward it while never looking up, until the great icon was before me. As I raised my eyes, there it was. Over 4,000 years old, this colossus stood with a full moon directly above it just like the photo from my studies. It offered the illusion that the moon's bright light had created a halo above its girth. Witnessing this boyhood dream before me, I was suddenly overcome with emotion. A short-lived feeling, it was to be. From out of the night's shadows stepped five armed men, faces so dark I could barely see anything but their piercing eyes. They quickly grabbed me and began to drag me toward Cheops. The only one of them who spoke English said, "It's much more fascinating inside."

There was something in the way he said it that I knew at that moment I was in trouble. In an attempt to remove myself from any danger I quickly shouted, "The Greeks built the Pyramids and the ancient Egyptians were the slaves." He translated what I said. At first, they looked confused, and then angry. They began screaming at me in Arabic. In a split second I saw an opening and dashed away toward the waiting cab. The chase began. In the distance, I could hear the siren of a police car approaching.

The police intercepted. Thank God the cabbie had called them. As I turned around, the eerie band of five had once again disappeared into the shadows of the Pyramid. The police lectured me on the dangers of the night, informing me that people have been known to disappear beneath the sands. Especially those who traveled alone. I was lucky to have escaped. They could smell I was a novice exploring foreign territories. Now, with one obstacle down, I knew it was only the beginning of a lifetime of journeys.

The next morning, my guide (a respected elder) took me to a tomb in Saqqara, also known as the "cemetery of the ancients." There lies its oldest structure, the Steppe Pyramid, built 5,000 years ago and a magnificent structure of the time. We had secured authorization to enter the newly discovered Royal Tomb of Mere, dated 2340 BC, that belonged to a high official of the Pharaohs. The musty smell of the air inside was prominent. And it felt familiar, even though I had not been there before. My guide mentioned that the noble's mummy had disappeared, likely destroyed in antiquity by robbers. There were about four rooms, but one in particular gave me a profound sense of knowing. I couldn't describe what I felt to my guide, but I wanted to be alone and have a meditation there. Permission was granted.

For half an hour I sat in the sand, and an extraordinary thing happened. As I came out of the meditation, I dug my hands in the sand beneath me and with one hand discovered an object wrapped in a mummified cloth. I carefully brought it to the surface, unwrapped it and found a young man's jaw that I estimated to be over 4,000 years old. Then, with my other hand dug deep into the ancient sands, I lifted out a beautiful necklace filled with semiprecious stones and encased in gold.

As I examined my treasures, I heard voices approaching. I didn't want to give up my discovery, so I buried the necklace quickly back into the sand and hid the mummified cloth under my armpit.

My guide arrived and I showed him what I had discovered. To my surprise he said, "Keep it, it belongs to you."

As we were driving away from the tomb, I further examined my treasure. Thoughts raced: Did it really belong to me? Had it waited all this time for me to bring it back into the light? Was it mine from another life? I had no answers.

I turned around and looked through the back window of the car, and with the great Steppe Pyramid getting smaller and smaller behind me, I began to sob. My guide asked what was wrong. I explained that I felt I was leaving behind a part of myself from the ancient past. He was moved. Upon leaving Cairo, I asked my guide how to get the find through customs. He told me to give him twenty dollars, which he in turn gave to the official, and I passed through promptly. We embraced and he quietly said, "I love that you love my country. Please come back, after all, you had lived here in a previous life. That was your discovery." What a wonderful way to finish this journey. It began with a threat and ended with a revelation.

As I navigated customs in New York the officer asked, "What the hell is that?"

"Family heirlooms," I replied, "one of my ancestors."

With a disgusted look on his face he said, "What, you have to live with this?"

"Yes. And I will have to pass it on to the next generation."

He quickly dismissed me and my treasure.

Ten years later I did return to the Tomb of Mere, but it had been thoroughly cleaned out, with no evidence of the necklace I had discovered and buried back into the sand.

Climbing Mount Sinai

Sitting on Mt. Sinai at dawn. (Author's Collection)

I read an article in the *Los Angeles Times* about some of the revelations people experienced when they climbed Mt. Sinai, the mountain where Moses had met God by the burning bush at the foot of the summit.

Ready for a new adventure, I called Louis Muchy, a spiritual teacher and friend who at sixty-two years of age had never left America. He agreed to make the trip with me, and like in ancient times, the master and the student, young and old, would explore it together.

We arrived at Cairo Airport and were embraced by what we thought were government officials, only to learn later they were travel agents. We arranged to have them meet us at the hotel foyer to receive our tickets to Sinai. Early that morning I was meditating while Louis was having breakfast downstairs. It always helped me start my day peacefully, before the onslaught of modern life. In Cairo, when crossing the street, you take your life into your own hands. As the Egyptians say, "If it is written, it is done."

In a subconscious state, I felt and saw something I had never experienced before. I lay frozen in a state of fear. I couldn't move my arms, let alone get up. An amazing

Tomb of Mere. (Author's Collection)

apparition appeared before me: a Pharaoh, wearing a bright golden headdress and with piercing painted eyes came at me over and over again. The face finally stopped, inches from mine, transfixed. It was frightening. Then flashes of golden rain came pouring into my being. My body jolted every time it came at me. I couldn't make a sound. I knew then that I was having an out-of-body experience. Then suddenly it disappeared. As I left the meditation I thought, *What the hell was that?* I was surprised that I had been under for almost an hour. I couldn't wait to tell Louis.

While visiting the archeological museum in Cairo that afternoon, a relief on a wall of the Pharaoh Akhenaten with golden rays pouring down on him stood out to me. Was he the one I saw coming at me in my meditation? And was the golden rain I felt the sun's rays pouring through me?

"That's him," I told Louis, who said he felt the Pharaoh in my meditation was preparing us for the climb and guiding us to the light.

Later that afternoon the travel agent met us in the hotel foyer to give us our travel arrangements for crossing the desert to Mt. Sinai. As I went to hand him my American Express card, it snapped in half between my two fingers. He jolted. The concierge, who had witnessed the incident from behind his desk, rushed over. He asked to see the travel agent's license, and with that the agent excused himself and bolted out. When the concierge examined the tickets, he told us we were about to be scammed. I felt we were being protected in this search for Moses' path. Along that road I realized that "the way through and the way out" would be met with obstacles and shadows.

The concierge recommended a new driver, and for six hours the next day we drove, passing by the Suez Canal and into the endless desert. I turned to my teacher and said, "This is the place where Moses guided his people to the Promised Land, and so are we on our own terms."

Louis replied, "That's what deserts are about, a place to be cleansed and renewed." It was a long drive but interesting to observe how the winds had sculpted this endless landscape.

That afternoon we arrived at a small hotel below Sinai made of ancient stones and blended into the face of the Sinai. A guide picked us up at 1 a.m. for the great trek up the Holy Mountain, which reaffirmed my belief that mountains are nature's monuments to man because they are closer to God.

We began the 7,500-foot ascent. We passed the great monastery of St. Catherine, built in the 6th century AD by the Emperor Justinian to protect the monks. Since its inception the monastery has never been without its believers. Even the

Inside Tomb of Mere. (Author's Collection)

St. Catherine's Monastery. (Author's Collection)

At the top of Sinai. (Author's Collection)

In memory of Louis Muchy. (Author's Collection)

Bedouins who roam and live in this environment are always there. It was wonderful to see Louis' first journey out of the United States at the site where the Ten Commandments were created by God's hand. His face was luminous.

The whole purpose of climbing at that hour, apart from avoiding the heat, was to arrive in time to witness God's holy light at dawn, creating new beginnings. Rather than riding a camel, we decided to walk the path as Moses did. Our guide was pleased. As Louis said, "The way to keep a trail alive is to walk on it."

As we walked along the very long and arduous rocky path, the bright light of the moon served as our ever-present guide. Almost every hour we would come across a Bedouin tent where tea was prepared for those making the pilgrimage.

Louis was a little nervous that at his age he might not be able to complete the steep journey. What kept him going was the privilege of climbing this treasured mountain, and by completing it he would become part of that heritage. Four hours and many steps later, Louis had to pause. He insisted that I continue without him. He said I could not miss out on the light that strikes you at dawn once you get to the top. Reluctantly, I left him with the guide and paced myself quickly to climb the last 375 steps leading to the top. It was exhausting, but the sun had not yet shown its face. I looked down to the end of the trail and spotted Louis walking slowly, on his terms. He seemed frail, so I ran down as fast as I could until I reached him. Exhausted from the effort, Louis fell on the rocky slope. Much to my dismay, the guide found it humorous. As I lifted Louis up, I told the guide he should have respect for his elders. He just shrugged, and I told him we did not need his services any longer. I was stunned by his attitude as he walked away, swearing in Arabic. But there are no mistakes and I felt strongly that we had to do this together, teacher and student. Slowly, painfully with each step, our feet aching, Louis trying to catch his breath, we finally reached our destination.

On the rocky top, walking on stones so ancient, we leaned against a tiny church. An old monk came out, chanting "Kyrie eleison, Kyrie eleison" and imparting blessings to us from God. In his nineties, the monk had to be carried all the way down to St. Catherine's monastery for the annual Feast of Bread to join all the other monks. It was the only time he went down. He was a true hermit.

Moments after the blessing, the powerful sun rose up over the mountains as it has for eons, with its golden rays embracing us. As I stood there, I remembered the cognition that happened in my hotel room where I felt the Pharaoh God Akhenaten hit me with his rays of gold, but now it was I who was experiencing my God's light with another revelation. We talked about it, sang hymns about it, and then Louis and I embraced each other because of it. We knew that we had made our pilgrimage in our time and on our own terms. We realized that to reach a sacred space in life one must voyage through the shadows, no matter how dark the light — and when it shines through you, the feeling is euphoric.

Louis Muchy died in 2007. I had taken him to Italy and Greece as well. He never forgot that first journey, as it inspired him to seek other worlds on his own. It made a difference at the end of his life's search when he quietly went into the light, shining. I miss him dearly.

Assisi

Lion eating a Christian at the Cathedral of St. Rufino, Assisi. (Author's Collection)

Sir John Mandeville once said, "If a man set out from home on a journey and kept right on going, he would come back to his own front door. It is when you come full circle, that you perceive the truth of that journey, that we gain a greater understanding of how we see life, the world, and God. And eventually, it will bring about change."

I always dreamed of visiting Italy, a country far different than any other culture. There is so much art, expressing life of the highest order. When in Rome I hired a guide to take me on a three-hour drive to Assisi, the Umbrian town in Italy. It was on my bucket list after seeing the Franco Zeffirelli film *Brother Son, Sister Moon* about the life of St. Francis.

I told my guide that I wanted to find the small church where St. Francis began his Franciscan Order by returning to Christ's own principles and rejecting the wealth and opulence of the medieval times. I explained the history of how St. Francis' friars lived in poverty, preaching barefoot in the streets of Assisi. This shocked the wealthy inhabitants of Assisi into shame. His creed was to live simply without the material trappings of daily life.

My driver apparently had no idea what I was talking about. It is curious to me that a journeyman such as myself sometimes has to explain the culture to those who live in it. He seemed quite exasperated with me and dumped me at a church to satisfy my passion. It was a huge domed basilica — Santa Maria degli Angeli — built in the 16th century and clustered around the Assisi station. I didn't think it was exactly what I was looking for, but what the hell, it was a start.

I walked through this enormous church and sat down to pray to the Virgin Mary that stood in front of me. As I opened my eyes and looked around, I noticed that in its center stood a small chapel. I walked over and began to read the contents of this small shelter embraced by frescoes of the saints. I could hear strains of a sermon coming from the inside the chapel. I walked into the small sheltered space, observing the other pilgrims as the father preached the gospel. It suddenly dawned on me that this chapel was ancient, so much older than the cathedral that housed it. My eyes wandered the walls as I struggled to determine the origins of it all.

As the priest began to offer the wafer, I began to tear. Could this be the small church I had been searching for? Indeed, it was. My guide had delivered me "by accident," thereby revealing another experience of trusting the process. This was the place of the earliest Franciscan movement. I was surrounded by 14th-century frescoes of the life of St. Francis in a small space secluded in the church's baroque bowels. I took the wafer from the priest and after the ceremony walked into the garden full of rose bushes. It was there on blooming rose bushes that St. Francis threw himself while grappling with immense nocturnal temptation. It was only after contact with his saintly flesh that the thorns dropped off.

Legend has it that the now thornless bushes bloom every May, their leaves stained with the blood shed by that night. St. Francis was proclaimed a saint only a few years after his death.

I visited the Basilica of St. Francis, where his remains are interred surrounded by

Giotto's magnificent frescoes, gloriously expressing the faith of Christianity. I peered through the metal bars to feel closer to his spirit. It was so close, yet I could feel only the empty space as my hands reached in. I went within and found my connection to this holy spirit. If you're going to open up, it might as well be with a trusted source. Again I realized that no matter what journey I took, somehow fate drew me to the sacred space of my quest, even if it seemed accidental. When such incidents occur, they appear like miracles that create God-like behavior, becoming one with the source. Again the concept of trust comes into play. It brought me back home, and I knew something had changed. Unexplainable, but walking in those footsteps the pilgrim keeps the path alive. And it is in those holy places that when we open our hand to God we receive his gifts.

In the Footsteps of Moses

Standing in the Roman ruins of Jerash, Jordan. (Author's Collection)

I wanted to further my expedition following the path of Moses. And so I took off across the Jordanian desert, beginning at the capital, Amman, then to Jerash and finally to the magnificent mountaintop of Mt. Nebo. From there I crossed the desert into the lost city of Petra with a ride through the Wadi Rum desert, where Lawrence of Arabia conquered Aqaba away from the Turks.

I arrived in Jerash (known as Antioch in ancient times), a beautifully preserved

Greco-Roman city where St. Paul lived and walked in the Bible. I passed the huge balustrade of columns lining the path where chariot indentations are clearly seen to the arched gateway that was built to celebrate Hadrian's visit in 129 AD.

In search of a guide, I came upon an area where thirty men sat puffing on cigarettes waiting for the next tourist to come by. Among the men there was only one woman, so I chose her. The puzzled expressions on the faces of the men were priceless as I passed them in favor of the sole female. Her name was Magda, and as we made our way out, she raised her head high, held her cigarette and smiled brightly. She was apparently very pleased I chose her over her male rivals and made a show of it. Meanwhile, the men held their worry beads in their hands, twirling them in agitation. She remarked, "When are males ever going to get over that the world is not always dedicated to them?"

Magda was a terrific guide with a wondrous sense of humor. Together we walked among the preserved ruins, among the best I've seen. We were transported 2,000 years back in time to the period after the Romans left and the Christians took over. We followed the track by the Persian invasion in 614 AD, followed by the Muslim conquest of 636 AD. A major earthquake in 749 AD seriously damaged the city and hastened its decline. It wasn't until 1806 that Jerash was rediscovered under the buried sand, which accounted for its remarkable preservation.

Tourists were scant and it seemed we had the place all to ourselves, except for the occasional looter who would secretly reveal ancient coins with the face of Alexander the Great. I was tempted to buy some, and as I held them in my hand I imagined the exchanges that took place centuries ago with these very coins. In the end I declined because without a legal receipt you could get arrested. My next destination was Mt. Nebo, situated eight hundred meters above the Jordanian Valley. Nebo provides a unique balcony for a bird's-eye view of the Holy Land. To the south, there lie the Dead Sea and the Desert of Judah, and to the west, the mountains of Judea and Samaria.

On top of this mount, history passed before me. It was a clear day, and in the far distance Bethlehem appeared in what remains of Herod's fortress and the oasis of Jericho. The ancient Christians had constructed a memorial church over ancient columns in honor of Moses. Six tombs had been found beneath the church. It is believed that Moses was buried here too, but his tomb has never been found.

I crossed the mosaic floor to the altar and lit a candle in memory of what had passed before me, and another to bless the next journey through Petra and the harsh Bedouin desert. As I was leaving the mountain, I glanced back to remember that it was here where Moses looked upon the land below and promised it as an inheritance for the chosen people. And what a view he had of the land he wandered in exile for

On top of Mt. Nebo overlooking Jordan Valley. (Author's Collection)

Drinking water at Moses' holy well. (Author's Collection)

Hadrian's Arch. (Author's Collection)

forty years. I picked up some sandy earth and felt it in my hands, thinking how he had walked these grounds, and wondering, "Where was Moses?"

Two and a half hours away was the city of Petra where Bedouins and their herds roam the endless desert. It is a place that has not changed since biblical times, except for the jarring appearance of trucks that had formed a line a mile long, delivering food and supplies to the allies in Iraq. I realized how close in proximity I was to this long war as I could hear the sounds of battle echoing through the air. We quickly sped through.

Just outside of Petra, my driver had a surprise for me and brought me to a quiet spot with no one around. Lying before me was the rock that Moses had tapped with his scepter to bring forth water for his people. The underwater spring still runs today.

I went slightly mad and splashed the water all over me, thinking and hoping I would be the willing recipient of this biblical and historical source of liquid benediction. I drank so much water, as much as I could, and for a short moment I truly felt something. I thought, *I am holy*. Ah, how encouraging the mind can be.

We began to descend into Petra, which in Greek means "the rock." Its name comes from approximately 300 BC when wealthy Bedouins carved an ancient city out of stone. Petra had been lost to the Western world for over five hundred years. It wasn't until the early 19th century when a Swiss explorer named Johann Ludwig Burckhardt heard the myth of this lost Nabataean civilization. Since it was a dangerous place for a Westerner to explore, he crafted a plan to study the Arabic language, bronze himself and then enter Egypt as an Indian Muslim. Befriending another Arab, Burckhardt's disguise convinced the Muslim he was one of them, and so he persuaded his new friend to take him through into Petra. He eventually brought light to this ancient world that had disappeared for many centuries.

It was in Petra that I found a Bedouin guide named Sulaman. I learned he was the eldest of nine children and responsible for his family as his father had been crippled in a motorcycle accident. We galloped on horseback from the beginning of the gorge through the Siq as Burckhardt had done in earlier times. It was a narrow mile-long passageway that eventually led to the cut-rock city of Petra. Upon entering this mythical place, buried from view but rising intact from the past, I was confronted by this extraordinary spectacle and glimpses of the lives of those who had created it. The strange thing about these hidden places, preserved for centuries, is that their mystery still haunts us even today. Only one percent of this civilization has been uncovered. In the winter months archaeologists are busy uncovering and deciphering, but it's a slow process.

Inside the ancient city of Petra. (Author's Collection)

Very little writing has been found among the ruins, which has helped keep the mystery alive. The merchants were wealthy because of their connection along the route of the Silk Road. I climbed everywhere from the Treasury to the ancient amphitheater and into the Roman area at the end of the road. I paused for a long time at the theatre, made of red stone. Like a member of an audience, I marveled at what my eyes could see. Nothing in all my travels compared to it. It was totally unique, empty of the inhabitants of its ancestral past, but its shell remained almost intact with colors gloriously seeping through stone, bringing its brilliance to life.

The next day we went into the Wadi Rum desert where we passed the Seven Pillars of Wisdom and then sat out the afternoon in a Bedouin tent, sipping mint tea while lounging around on cushions like sheiks. We exchanged stories of respective history. I learned why Bedouins constantly move, and they in turn got a glimpse of life in America. They revealed very little about themselves but played their reservations with charm. I discovered that Bedouins move because of their animals, and finding a location shaded from the heat was necessary in this red, endless desert. Living in this harsh environment with so little to distract them, I'm sure there was substantial inward search about their rituals to Allah and the frugalities of a nomad's life. I informed them that we have many poor people in America as well, but we have great freedom as individuals that money can't buy. They were surprised. I was thrilled living the unknown.

My journey ended with an enlightening experience. Sulaman drove me back to Amman and I invited my Bedouin friend for lunch at the Four Seasons Hotel. Dressed in his traditional garb and wearing a red and white keffiyeh over his head, we entered the restaurant. And what an entrance it was. The concierge freaked as he looked upon Sulaman with disdain. He tried to block his way, while I objected and told him to behave himself. He froze and Sulaman smiled. Then we sat ourselves in the lovely Italian restaurant. He admired the beautiful flowers and the table setting that Bedouins never see in the desert. This new experience led him to become animated in a way he never had been in his sheltered world. The hotel employees stood looking aghast as we enjoyed a wonderful lunch and laughed at their ignorance.

The extraordinary irony about this journey was that although Sulaman was a direct descendant of the creators of Petra, those who now lived off its glory wanted to exclude him from his heritage. But for this one day he reconnected with the wealth of his past. I left Jordan knowing that I had shared a profound slice of time with a truly amazing man.

Entrance to Petra. (Author's Collection)

Transitions

It was the end of summer, and the sun was gloriously fading as I landed at the Athens airport in Greece. I had just finished reading Homer's epic poem *The Odyssey* on the plane, and by the end of that visual saga I felt I had actually lived the magical experience of time travel, going back to the source.

Now I was returning to my ancient home like a Homeric spirit who had come

Entering Petra at the Treasury, a tomb that made this icon famous. (Author's Collection)

back to the womb after a long absence in a distant land. I had been invited by some Greek producers interested in developing a series based on a lawyer's true experiences exposing corrupt officials in Europe. I loved the idea of playing a spy and in the language of my ancestors, and for my parents, a dream come true.

Usually I make sure I'm cleaned up before disembarking, because you never know what relative lurks at Greek airports or when the occasional photographer is nearby, seeking a candid version of me. My life in show business has meant never letting the public see you unless it looks like you just jumped out of a television set or a movie studio.

Well, not all the time. That wouldn't be normal.

But that was my training, and I thought it best that I change in the bathroom before exiting the terminal as I was going straight to a meeting arranged by my journalist friend Alkinos Bounias.

As I exited the plane and stepped down outside of the terminal, a dozen Greek reporters ran at me with Alkinos in tow. Their cameras flashing, microphones stretched out, blurting out passionate questions about Greek affairs. "What do you have to say about Greece and Macedonia?"

All I could think was, the last time I looked in the mirror my hair was standing up stick-straight and I was still wearing the clothes I'd slept in, and certainly was not ready for a close-up. Pulling myself together like the part required, I happened to have in my carry-on bag a book about Vergina, a place in ancient Macedonia where Alexander the Great and his father Philip the Second had lived. By coincidence I had picked up that copy in the United States as I had become fascinated with Alexander's beginnings and the places he chose to conquer. How appropriate, I thought, and how bloody lucky.

So I pulled that rabbit out of a hat and flaunted the book in front of their cameras and calmly replied, "Macedonia is Greek, read your history." The cameras flashed and the journalists went crazy. Forgetting I was wearing overalls and was disheveled, I answered their questions with relish and abandon. It made the front page and the evening news, and so did my hair. They were impressed that a foreign Greek knew more about their history than they did, and an actor no less. I love smashing myths about actors being dumb. God was watching.

The next evening a dinner had been set up with a commercial producer and his wife. Alkinos and I arrived early and had a chance to catch up and strategize. He was a respected journalist with his own afternoon talk show that played upon his wacky humor. It was not unusual for guests to enter through a refrigerator door and

Walking through the Siq, Petra. (Author's Collection)

be interviewed by Alkinos from his bed. It was an original setting where he could be lethal and at times hysterical with a temperament that could explode through the roof. But we got along well, except when he was chain-smoking cigarettes. Then his tone would get sharper and at times illogical. He was dark-featured, so that made it all the more dramatic. But behind all this façade, Alkinos had a heart of gold — you just had to find a way through.

The *Mission: Impossible* series I had starred in during the early '90s was such a great success that Mega Channel in Greece had repeated the episodes for years. Because of that, this dinner was set up to discuss my playing a James Bond character in a commercial for Drambuie liquor. We enjoyed a delicious and expensive dinner, the atmosphere was relaxed and it gave me a chance to discuss the subject in Greek. Everyone seemed delighted.

By now all the details of the commercial were put on the table. The product was presented with style, and the action sounded exhilarating. We all agreed that the concept was quite exciting. Then talk turned toward compensation, and what was left for me — a one-time buyout — was simply embarrassing. Alkinos froze and the producer and his wife had put on a mask. Talk of money does tend to change dynamics when fiscal agendas differ. I sat there dumbfounded. There was no discussion. No argument about how insulting the offer was. Just a take-it-or-leave-it deal.

I was in the throes of "business, Greek style."

Alkinos excused himself, allegedly to visit the restroom. Instead he headed straight to the maitre d', whom he knew well, and quietly asked him for a favor. He returned to our table, and within ten minutes the waiter arrived and handed the producer the bill. Reluctantly the producer accepted the hefty check, and Alkinos, in a manner fit for a king, elegantly said, "Thank you so much, me next time."

The producer was not happy. No deal and stuck with the check. Not the outcome he'd envisioned. We made uncomfortable small talk while he paid the bill, and then we unceremoniously parted ways, disappointed that there was no exciting commercial but reveling in Alkinos' resourcefulness and desire to forge ahead. In typical Greek fashion, Alkinos was already moving on to the next big thing as we stepped outside the restaurant. "Tomorrow we see producer Liana Patera for a film, and then Saturday evening the head of Mega Channel wants to take you to dinner to discuss a series called *The Red Stamp*."

As promised, the next day we visited Liana Patera in her office located below the ancient Acropolis. An attractive fair-haired woman in her mid-40s and very professional, Liana was a respected producer who survived in a male-dominant society.

With Alkinos Bounias at Meteora, Greece. (Author's Collection)

Celebrating with Alkinos in Athens. (Author's Collection)

The story she was producing was in the process of being written, taking place during the Second World War in Turkey where the protagonist was being held prisoner. She wanted her sister, an actress, to play my love interest. She also wanted to have the writer incorporate her observations of my personality into the character. Animatedly, she told us the war story with passion. "Greeks love tragedy," she explained. "And why not, we invented it."

We shared ideas about how it would end, and then the question of salary came up. Again we were shocked. "That is insulting," Alkinos responded. He explained my popularity in Greece and the fact that my appeal was international. He played it well, and I actually laughed out of embarrassment because in the U.S., deals were made without the actor present. She explained her predicament with the budget, but still Alkinos passed.

He told her, "We have great interest from Mega Channel. On Saturday they invited us out to dinner." This piqued her interest, but Alkinos was reluctant to go into details.

Once again another opportunity to work in Greece fell through because of an unacceptably low offer. I thanked her and wished her well on the film, but her expression revealed suppressed anger. I smiled and we parted. "Next meeting," I told Alkinos, "issues on salary are not to be discussed in front of me — it makes me uncomfortable, and it's unprofessional." He agreed.

It was early Friday morning, and I wanted to shift the dynamics by visiting what I loved most, an ancient historic place that spoke back to me. I had adventured into Troy and read many books on the subject, so I wanted to see the city of Mycenae, where the archaeologist Heinrich Schliemann discovered the Royal Shaft Tombs of Greek kings and warriors of the Trojan War. It all began there, and it took the Greeks ten years and many lives to destroy their Trojan enemy. He first discovered Troy in the 1870s because of his unshakable belief in the words of Homer, whose poems were a map to finding Troy. He did it in the same way when he uncovered the Citadel of Mycenae and Tiryns, completing the circle of all those involved in the Great War, and by doing so opened up a new world of archaeology. The world was paying attention. He found spectacular treasures, including golden death masks, weaponry and even the preserved remains of kings that disintegrated before his eyes. It's a great history, and I was grateful that I had read Homer's *The Iliad* and *The Odyssey* before coming here. Now I was prepared to witness it for myself, just as I did in Troy.

Early the next morning I hired a driver to pick me up and take me to the northeast part of the Peloponnese in Argolis, two hours outside of Athens. It was a beautiful ride through pine forests on rocky landscapes passing through the amazing Corinthian canal, which separates mainland Greece with the Peloponnese and is called the Isthmus. It was an idea and dream that started over 2,000 years ago and was completed in the 19th century. This narrow canal was created so that ships saved several days of sailing around the Peloponnesian landscape. It was a marvel of construction. Now we continued on to Mycenae and into the world of Homer's myths.

Mycenae was the center of power in the Late Bronze Age (1600–1100 BC). I could see this as I walked along the path of ruins, with the Lion's Gate standing in front of me as it had for thousands of years. Two lions sculpted into ancient stone stood on top of its entrance. The monolithic stone walls dominated the setting. What phenomenal memories of history must have been absorbed in those walls! Its culture was the source of epics and legends, the labors of Hercules, the Trojan War, and Agamemnon's tragic life and death. Now it all appeared calm. As I entered through the gate I could see the excavated ruins that Schliemann and his Greek wife Sophia had discovered on top of the rocky hill protected by these Cyclopean walls.

I explored the hill and landed in one of the Bronze Age burial sites. I laid down where Agamemnon may have been buried in a great ritual, filled with treasures fit for the great warrior and king. When Schliemann discovered this as the Tomb of Agamemnon with his golden mask and weapons of great artistry, he proclaimed this as the Greek king himself, who led Greece with a thousand ships to Troy.

After Schliemann's death it was discovered it belonged to another age, five hundred years earlier. At one point the bodies uncovered kept disintegrating into dust. Learning from this, Schliemann had brought some lacquer and sprayed the last body with it. Miraculously it held together. Upon hearing about this, the villagers carried the royal soldier through the town in respect of who he was in their long history.

I thought it an interesting story, so when I went back to the archaeological museum in Athens, I asked the officials, "What happened to the body?"

They had no idea what I was talking about. I loved Schliemann's story even though in his day they called him a dreamer, a man who improvised on history, a liar, a fraud and brilliant. Whatever he was, he did make a difference.

Since the Greek officials denied him a wing in the museum acknowledging his finds, he swept out the Trojan treasure and donated it to Germany, his country of birth. During the Second World War, the treasure disappeared. But fifty years later it was turned up in the basement of the Pushkin Museum in Russia by two curators — Akinsha and Koslov. They brought it to the world's attention along with millions of other pieces of art, regarded as war booty.

The Russians had no choice but to put it on display in 1994, while Greece, Turkey and Germany demanded the treasure back. The Russians ignored their demands, and why not? The treasure's worth is about one billion dollars today, whereas the Mycenaean haul has remained in Athens. Those haunting golden masks are so alive and so beautifully executed during the zenith of the Mycenaean culture.

I walked around in the hot sun, searching for some overlooked treasure waiting for me to find. I didn't have to claim anything as my own; for me the discovery alone was the prize. Searching among the ruins I found many pieces of pottery, felt them, talked to them and left them where they landed. What Schliemann must have felt uncovering all these jewels that had waited for him to discover. One can only dream.

It was a great day navigating the beehive-shaped tombs and all the citadels overlooking the Mycenaean landscape. While taking a sandwich break, I thought about how archaeologists had worked on these puzzles, putting all of the pieces together. To the average visitor the walls remained silent, and what an eerie silence it was. It is left to one's imagination the tragedies that unfolded here, where in the heart of the palace Agamemnon was murdered by his wife Clytemnestra and her lover after he returned victorious from the Trojan War. What's left are just the grey ruins scarred for ages by the weather.

It was a wonderful respite, exploring the richness of the history firsthand. But back to business at hand: I received a nice surprise when I met a Greek actress who was one of the most beautiful people I had ever seen.

Mimi Denisi had her own theatre and school where she provided training for the country's youth. We went out for dinner and exchanged histories and laughed at the triumphs and tribulations that lived in our profession. She had enjoyed great success on the London stage and was a superstar of Greece. She told me there would be no press around, so we could quietly get to know each other. But after an hour, fourteen journalists and photographers barged in with lights flashing. Mimi played the innocent card, but after all, any story that lands on the front page was worth lying about. I loved our times together.

It was time to go back to Athens and have an early night, to be rested for the next evening's Mega Channel dinner. Before work or taking meetings, I always made it a point to fill my mind and spirit with great history. That always fed my passion to excel.

Dinner with beautiful Greek actress Mimi Denisi. (Author's Collection)

Alkinos and I met with our group of professionals at a wonderful new restaurant in Athens. There were ten of us, with me sitting at the head of the table and Mega Channel bigwig George Andreas directly opposite. In his finely tailored suit, Andreas was an imposing man — bald, rich and in his mid-60s. On my left was an ordinary but highly intelligent man wearing heavy glasses whose character I was to portray in *The Red Stamp*. He was fascinating, a lawyer challenging European democracies with a strong pen, exposing their clandestine cover-ups whilst he lived the life of a spy. He loved *Mission: Impossible*, and he was thrilled I would portray him in the series, mostly because we spoke the same language. He thought of us as old friends. The rest were publicity people, their wives and a couple of producers. Alkinos sat next to the bigwig so he could draw out as much information from him about the impending deal and when the series would be shot.

In the middle of dinner Mr. Andreas blurted out, "How much money are we looking at?"

A little surprised after my mandate to Alkonis to not address such things in my presence when the previous meetings had gone south during financial talks, I replied, "I don't discuss money over the dinner table."

"Well, just give me a clue," he said.

"No," I retorted.

The table was silent for the first time. We just stared at each other. Breaking the tension, I said, "You remind me of my uncle."

"Did you love your uncle?" he asked.

"No," I said. Not everyone was laughing.

At that moment Liana Patera, the producer we had previously met, crashed the dinner party. She came straight up to me with a beautifully wrapped gift and kissed me on both cheeks.

Hmm, I thought, Greeks bearing gifts. What was she up to?

She greeted everyone at the table and kissed Mr. Andreas on both cheeks as well, whispered something in his ear and disappeared like a fleeing ghost. Alkinos looked at me and then suspiciously looked Patera's way. Perturbed, George Andreas stared at me for a moment and said, "I thought you were making your debut in Greece with us? Patera just told me she got you first and got you cheap."

I was shocked and insulted, but I held back my anger. For the first time I finally understood the meaning of "beware of Greeks bearing gifts." Its origin took place during the Trojan War, when the famous wooden horse filled with Greek warriors, created by the crafty Ulysses, was presented to the enemy as a parting gift. By accepting and bringing it into its sacred grounds, Troy was destroyed by fire, and Greece had its glory.

Alkinos quickly jumped in, proclaiming it was a lie, and then looked to me, wondering if I had made a secret deal with Patera behind his back.

I stared the big honcho right in the eye and said, "Alkinos is correct. But let me be truthful here, the past few days I have experienced how you do business here. I'm not impressed and I don't come cheap. Doing this series will not change my career. I wanted to do something Greek for my parents. I want to thank you and everyone for dinner, but it's time for me to go."

I shook hands and departed. They all objected in vain. Two hours later, Alkinos was screaming on the phone, accusing me of betraying him after all he had done. I never forgot that experience and that gift, which was a beautiful gold clock. It has remained in my closet to always remind me how untrustworthy people can be — with kisses and an empty smile.

That night I didn't sleep well, but I had a dream in the early morning that changed my life. I woke up in a sweat, feeling that something was wrong with my family, specifically my mother. In my dream she was climbing a stairway where her mother who had passed years earlier was reaching out for her. I called Australia right away and discovered that her cancer had returned, and she was given only months to live.

I sobbed for hours. I didn't answer the phone even though it kept ringing; I was not interested in playing those games anymore. My trip home to Greece turned out to be hardly Homeric. Something more important was calling, and I had to get back before my mother made her transition. I packed and left on the next plane to Sydney. With the exception of Alkinos, my path never crossed with those Greeks again even though they kept calling, trying to seduce me with new ideas. The bad taste that was left lasted a long time, and it took many years for me to return.

With my parents at their house in Sydney. (Author's Collection)

I arrived in Sydney where my brother picked me up and drove me straight to the hospital. My mother had lost a great deal of weight, and my father, who was not known as an affectionate man, was beside himself. He belonged to that Victorian-era mindset where men remained reserved and emotions were held tight. My sisters, Connie and Pauline, arrived and we stayed close to each other for strength. The whole family loved her dearly. Mother always had a sense of humor, but the life she had lived with my father was difficult, as Greek men didn't always respond to their partner's needs.

My mother often brushed my father aside for her kids, especially me since I was her oldest son. I always believed he resented me for that. She always worried about me being away from her in America, while my father in his temperamental tantrums blamed her cancer on my long absence.

But now we gathered together to attend to her needs. I sat massaging her feet and hands and told her of my experiences in Greece. She took all her energy to laugh, calling them "a bunch of crooks." I held her as long as I could until the doctor came in to check her condition. She wasn't responding to the new drugs and her lungs were filling up with fluid. The relatives were sitting in the waiting room, all looking sad.

The next day I went to a furniture store and bought her a new bedroom suite. I told my siblings that when she was released from the hospital she should have something to look forward to, and they all loved the idea. We gave the old furniture to Goodwill, and when the new furniture arrived my father became emotional. That was a rare experience. I saw he had a heart after all. I went back to see my mother as I wanted some time alone with her in case she passed. My relatives' despondent faces revealed they could see the end coming. I wanted to lift up her spirits and have her feel that death was not a closed door, that she had things to look forward to. Like seeing America and Greece again.

She always smiled when she saw me, especially when I brought her papayas, healthy salads and soup. The chemotherapy was cutting down her appetite and her cancer was spreading. After I told her about her new bedroom suite, she glowed. I described it in detail knowing her spirits would stay elevated.

When I spoke of my latest journey to the Middle East, she always would have the same response: "Aren't you ever afraid?" I would always laugh. She loved hearing about the spiritual places, because her "God beliefs" gave her strength. When I told her about lighting candles in her name in sacred places where the Holy Family passed through or in Jerusalem at the spot where the Christ was born, her eyes would light up and tear. Faith had its connection there, and through me she found a link.

After a long afternoon, the doctor took me aside and kindly told me they had done all they could.

"What does that mean?" I asked.

"Well, I think she would be more comfortable in a hospice now," he replied.

When he left I thought, *Isn't that a place where people go to die?*

Concerned and still in denial, I said goodbye to Mother as there were some relatives waiting to see her. As I was leaving, my cell phone rang. It was my older sister, Connie, telling me that my father had had a heart attack and he was in another hospital in the eastern suburbs. I caught a cab and rushed to see him. My family was

My father's parents and sisters. (Author's Collection)

My brother George and sister Connie visit me in Los Angeles. Monk painting by Enrique Senis-Oliver. (Author's Collection)

already there. "What is happening to us?" was written on their worried faces. As I approached the room I could hear my father telling the nurses about me. I entered the room slowly, and from his bed he pointed at me with pride, "That's my son." How time heals. He was glowing at the nurses, and they smiled back at him with joy.

I was told he had had a mild heart attack and would have to remain in the hospital for just a few more days for observation. Of course my father asked about mother, and the thought of her leaving began to wear on him. After sixty years of marriage perseverance had prevailed and so had love. We enjoyed a heartfelt exchange, and he thanked me for sending them overseas so many times. He said that my work had enriched both of their lives.

I thought, *Let the past go* — after twenty years of spiritual counseling about mental and physical abuse, it is forgiveness that lets all that baggage go.

We embraced and he assured me he would be fine, but not to tell my mother as she had too much on her plate. I told him that I was leaving in a couple of days because of work but that I would return as soon as I could. As I was leaving, he asked, "How did you know your mother was ill?"

"I saw her in a dream with Grandma, waiting for her," I replied.

"God must be talking to you. That's good, maybe it's a blessing," he responded.

I looked at him carefully and I smiled. The look of regret was on his face. Without doubt, he allowed himself to really see me for the first time.

I noticed that my female relatives waiting in the hall all looked defeated, as if the paths chosen for them didn't quite parallel the journeys they came to fulfill. Male dominance and the quiet power of mothers didn't allow them to finish their education, because in our culture a woman's purpose was to marry and help raise their children. By the looks on their faces, love was not permeating through their lives, as if they asked themselves the question "This is it?" And sometimes I caught them looking in my direction with a critical eye, wondering how I got away and did it on my own. I suppose I was an enigma to them; I was the first Greek male in his youth who left his family in Australia and succeeded without them, against their judgments and dismissals.

"He left a failure, he'll come back a failure," one once said.

My immediate family had to deal with it until I proved all of them wrong. The wait was long as my pursuit was not an overnight success.

I returned to my mother, knowing that none of us had any intention of letting her know about Father's condition. An ambulance was to pick her up and take her to the hospice.

With my parents at Universal Studios. (Author's Collection)

With Mum and siblings in Circular Quay, Sydney. (Author's Collection)

As they were carrying her out, she looked at me and said in Greek, as always, "Are you riding along with me?"

"Well, of course," I replied as I held her hand.

We drove off and I will never forget that expression in her eyes; she felt safe at that moment. That lovely face looked haunted as a result of the disease. Fifteen minutes later she lay in a hospice room, wondering what was next.

"Why hasn't your father come to see me?" she asked.

I covered my emotions and told her he thought it best to stay home, as too many visitors would tire her out. She accepted it and I excused myself to go to the bathroom.

When I returned, a nurse was carrying a tray with ice cream into my mother's room. I pulled her aside to explain that ice cream should not be given to patients with my mother's disease as it fed the cancer.

She bluntly replied, "Your mother has ten days to live. Let her enjoy her last moments."

Stunned, I was lost for words. Nobody had bothered to convey that to me. I sat with my mother for another hour as I watched her eat the ice cream. I told her quietly that I had to leave that evening as I had to be on set in two days.

She lovingly touched my face and said, "Thank you for coming from so far away. My little boy, who had pennies in his pocket and grew up to be rich."

"I will see you soon, Mama, please wait," I said.

We held each other for a while and I kissed her goodbye. I prayed that this was not our last time together. I cried all the way home. Late that afternoon I sat with my brother and sisters exchanging ideas on how to proceed in case our parents died.

My brother George was a schoolteacher, and a good one at that, happily married to Helen with two wonderful sons. My sisters were great, but part of the old regime that never allowed them to have their own careers, especially when they both excelled at school. With marriages arranged they certainly had reasons for regret. But their husbands, part of the old school, reflected the same beliefs. Certainly the doubts were there, always reminding me that I was a man, and therefore free to make my own decisions. If only they knew what it took, the struggle I went through to survive New York and Hollywood as an Australian Greek with a strange accent. It took a while for all of it to come together, and as a wise man told me, "Perseverance wins out."

The front door opened and there was my father standing with open arms to say goodbye. He didn't want to miss that opportunity. We gasped, and he told us that he let himself out of the hospital as he was feeling fine. I kissed him on both cheeks and scolded him for his careless action. He dismissed it, and I spent my last hour in

Sydney talking about our mother without telling him what the nurse had revealed. He seemed concerned that she would leave him behind.

It was interesting to see what happens when you get older and handle the inevitable face of death when it is in front of you. He again told me how he loved the new bedroom and how our mother would be sitting up proudly, like a queen. He couldn't wait for her to see it. I hugged him and my siblings, and as I turned back I remember thinking I should have held on to him a little longer.

My parents' wedding, November 17, 1940. (Author's Collection)

It was difficult leaving them behind, but my plane took off for the U.S. and I had plenty of time to think of all that had transpired. The Machiavellian Greeks and the beauty of their history all seemed unimportant in contrast with those human elements that we were all experiencing. The loss of your parents happens but once, and now it was our turn to face this common tragedy. I quickly immersed myself in my work. Every time a scene ended that first day back on set, my mind would move to the family in Australia. But while performing I learned to not waste those feelings that kept surfacing. I used my heavy emotions, filtering them through the dialogue and finding a creative way to release them.

That evening I got a call from my sister Connie — Dad had had a massive heart attack and was in serious condition in the hospital. Within the next hour my other sister Pauline called to say he had passed away. She had witnessed the moment he had the heart attack. It had been massive and had thrown him against the wall, where he suffered a bad gash on his forehead.

"At least he wasn't alone," I said.

The inevitable had happened. "At the end of the week I will be back home. Make sure Mum doesn't find out," I told my sister.

I hung up and unleashed a howl. I slipped onto the kitchen floor, where I sat for two hours. My mind kept racing. I was mainly concerned for my mum, but the way in which my father had died so violently upset me deeply. Did he let himself out of the hospital because he wanted to say goodbye to his children, standing on two feet, whole, that he knew his time was coming? But what of his wife Eva, how did he finish that? It was not over.

For the next four days I checked my service to make sure the family was holding together, and thought how difficult it must have been for them to be in our mother's presence and not reveal our father's passing. That last day before I left work I checked my messages, but there were none. Within that half hour of getting home they had called. The message was: Mother died quietly, never knowing her husband had passed away. I was numb. But something strange had taken place. While my sister Connie was giving my mother some water, she commented that it tasted bitter. As my sister turned to get her something else to drink, she heard my mother call out, "Agapitos." That was the Greek name for Peter. Connie turned and found my mother looking up at the ceiling with her eyes wide open; she had passed on, and my father had come to take her with him. Those next fourteen hours of flying back to Sydney were the longest I had ever known. We were to bury both of our parents together.

My brother met me at the airport, and we went straight to his house where the rest of the family was waiting. As soon as I embraced my sisters, whatever emotions they had held back now surfaced. Everyone broke down. That night we went to a common ritual before the church service and burial where our parents were put on display so the families could pay their last respects. It was an unbelievable and solemn ceremony.

After having lost so much weight, my mother's face had been filled in to give her a better appearance. The makeup was overdone and I hardly recognized her. Still, I wanted to cry out, but I thought of Patera's comment in Greece, "Greeks love tragedy, and why not, they invented it." Suddenly some humor bubbled to the surface. I was

Mum and her first son, me. (Author's Collection)

not about to fulfill that cliché. My father was ice cold when I kissed him, and the scar caused by the hard fall was still prominent on his forehead. It was the evidence of how he had died that late afternoon in February.

Everyone took turns in their final goodbyes, muttering their personal words and bringing a final comfort. It was the last time we would see my parents. I thought perhaps they left together to prepare a life for us on the other side when it came time for our transitions. But now I kept thinking, *With their souls carrying them to the other side, where do they go?* A couple of months later I would find out.

The day of the funeral, my favorite uncle, Bill, grabbed a cigarette out of my mouth and tossed it to the ground, stamped it out and cried, "That disease is what's killing all of us." Before I could respond, two hearses arrived together in front of my parents' house. That visual has stayed with me my entire adult life. It was so shocking a reality that I had to be excused. The church service was packed with friends and relatives. I don't remember much except the two coffins were closed, immersed in flowers, and the sermon by the priest where he proclaimed, "Their unusual love was the reason they left together."

I think my father died first because he was afraid to be left alone. My mother was exhausted and it was her heart that finally gave out before the cancer killed her. People came to the front of the church to pay their respects. I shook a lot of hands, as did my brother and sisters. While I was waiting outside the church a cousin came up to give his condolences, at the same time telling me about his struggles and how ten thousand dollars would help him out. At that moment my brother interrupted us. I looked my cousin straight in the eye and said, "The reason you're struggling is because your timing sucks. You don't listen." We left him to ponder his inappropriate behavior. We carried the coffins into the hearse and left for the final ceremony at Botany Bay cemetery.

Standing beside a large hole, the priest recited the final sermon. The ritual of lowering them down on top of each other, and the soil being shoveled in with a thud, sealed their final outcome. I was the last to leave. I struggled to tell them stories I couldn't even remember now. There was no euphoria of going to a better place, just a new sense of knowing that only comes to you after your parents have gone. The relatives came back to my parents' house and ate with us as a celebration of their life together.

Three days later I had to leave as new scenes were being written into the show I had just left. I was expected to be on set that next Monday. I said my goodbyes, leaving everyone to quietly persevere with their own pain and eventual healing. In the years that followed I would still reach for the phone to call my parents when good news had crossed my path. But that was just one of many things that happened that automatically recalled my parents. Television shows, especially ones dealing with a son's relationship to father and mother, opened up the floodgates.

Work was going very well until I was suddenly called to my producer's office to be told my character was being killed off. My producer was perplexed by my lackadaisical attitude, and I wasn't about to give them the expected response — that of an actor defeated. I left feeling free with no obligations except to seek the person who could give me an answer to my question "Where did my parents go?"

I eventually found a man named Ray Lingini who apparently was capable of reaching those who had crossed over. He was an Italian from New Jersey in his late thirties. One afternoon I sat with him in a guesthouse in Hollywood, where he began a foreign-sounding chant. On the table that separated us was a bottle of rum, some beads and a cigar.

Interesting recipe, I thought.

His body started to shake and a deep voice of a female spirit came through. He took the rum into his mouth and sprayed it all around me. He did this a number of times to clear the negatives. Then in a female manner lit the cigar and out came this roar.

"Who are Eva and Peter?"

Before I could answer, "she" responded in a Jamaican accent. I went totally quiet.

"They are on the other side. Your mother went through a lot of pain and is exhausted. Who is Maria, because she is holding your mother in her arms to comfort her?"

Maria was my mother's sister who had died a year before from leukemia. I couldn't say anything because emotions were erupting. "Peter is sitting on a bench looking very sad because he did not support his son through his youth and now he is grounded, somewhere between here and the spiritual world. In order to make his transition, he needs you to wear his ring, and that way he can connect and guide you in the coming years. It's for you to help him pay the price for not having fulfilled his destiny. He apologizes and loves you very much."

It all made so much sense. I was happy to understand and know that we all have another place to go — that death is just a transition where the soul is able to go back and exist in peace with its lessons learned, and that karma is a law that comes at a price. I felt sad for my father's lonely place but elated that my mother was safe. I left content that I had been guided to the right place. The amazing thing was that he actually knew their names, and that gave me a strange satisfaction. I called my family and told them of my experience. It brought them some peace of mind maybe believing that life was an ongoing process that didn't end in a coffin.

My mother and my Uncle Bill in 1930s Sydney. (Author's Collection)

My brother sent me my father's ring, and I haven't taken it off since. I sometimes find myself unconsciously touching it, and wonder if he is around me, fulfilling his karma. After that, I did not work for three years. I felt it was just so stupid, this game of disguise that was my profession for the past thirty years. My success was based on rescuing my parents and seeking their approval for having abandoned them in my early life. It was always for them but never for me.

Now I was faced with finally looking at myself. I felt a void. I was full with knowledge but with an emptiness of not knowing where to put it. It took a few years to fully process this for my own understanding. It came through when I was ready. The day I awoke was the day I was asked to come back to the show where my character had been killed off, after my parents' death. These were the transitions I had to go through to have a better understanding of change.

Coming Full Circle

Those heroes that shed their blood and lost their lives,
You are now lying in the soil of a friendly country.
Therefore rest in peace, there is no difference between the
Johnnies and the Mehmets to us where they lay side by side,
here in this country of ours,
You, the mothers, who sent their sons from faraway countries,
Wipe away your tears;
Your sons are now lying in our bosom and are in peace.
After having lost their lives on this land they have become our
Sons as well.

—Ataturk, 1934

It was a winter's dawn in Istanbul when I began my six-hour drive to Gallipoli in January of 2009. Being an Australian I went to pay homage to the lost souls of World War I, where thousands of Australian and New Zealand soldiers had perished. Such a stupid war, I thought, but some wars are necessary. The bravery of those men

This photo truly depicts how I felt at the funeral. (Sotos Kappas)

all began in the waters of the Dardanelles and ended there in January of 1916. So many died in vain, and by losing hundreds of thousands of young warriors Australia's population became affected.

The day was bitterly cold and raining so hard that the conditions seemed appropriate for the drama I was about to encounter. I stood in front of the epitaph left behind by Ataturk (1881–1938), Turkey's military commander and statesman and a towering figure of the 20th century. Not many have achieved so much in so short a period, from decisively transforming the life of a nation to the profound inspiration he gave to the rest of the world.

One of his great reforms was the emancipation of women and putting an end to the antiquated Ottoman dynasty, whose tale had lasted six centuries. During the 1920s he made the world take notice as a victorious commander who defeated his enemies. The world's nations honored him as a leading peacemaker who upheld the principles of humanism and the vision of a united humanity.

During this campaign (1915–1916) Ataturk was responsible for stopping the advance of the Allied Forces intent on capturing Istanbul. He commanded from the front lines with great courage and was hailed a war hero. Before his untimely death in 1938 he spearheaded his country's economic recovery, and without him there would have been no modern Turkish Republic. And that's why he was given the name Ataturk, meaning "Father of the Turks."

I was moved by the words he left behind posted on a billboard for all to see. It was called "The Gentleman's War" because of the great care each side took of its wounded enemy. By the time I read the hundreds of epitaphs on the simple gravestones with those haunting words by mothers in memory of their sons, I felt as if someone close to me had died. I was sobbing by the end, but the rain running down on my face hid my true emotions. It was all so simply set, even the ripple of the sea hitting the banks was too calm for such a setting.

I imagined what it was like for the Allies when they landed and charged up that steep hill, being shot down like animals, one after another. I ran to the top, to see how they must have been exposed. The terrain was used as a weapon by the Turks that helped them win the war. Three hundred soldiers were killed every fifteen minutes. Due to the nature of the landscape, the Allies couldn't see the targets and the objectives they wanted to achieve.

Gallipoli with my friend Sheri Anderson. (Author's Collection)

As I saw it, there was no chance of surviving — it must have been brutal. I was reminded of Peter Weir's great film *Gallipoli*. As I walked through the fields I could envision the skeletal remains of soldiers across the landscape where they fought and died. They rotted where they had fallen with no ceremony. Churchill, England's great leader, retired, and that huge loss would haunt him for the rest of his life.

My thoughts were interrupted by a busload of Australian tourists. They too had come to pay homage to the fallen. The rain had stopped as they exited the bus. I couldn't help but notice they were moved by what they saw. I was impressed they'd come so far to pay their respects. I heard a few begin conversing about Troy, pointing across the Dardanelles where the ancient battle between the Greeks and Trojans had been fought. I had visited there a couple of times before, and sat in the ruins imagining the cries of war echoing across the Troad, when the great fortress of Ilium was destroyed by fire. How many battles through history had been fought on this peninsula? It has been inhabited and embraced by an unbroken chain of civilizations since the dawn of mankind, each putting a stamp on their existence.

Now these wars of the past helped me recall my own history. My Greek ancestral tree began in the 15th century when Istanbul was still Constantinople. They were merchants who eventually moved to an island called Kastellorizo, two miles from the Turkish mainland. That's where my parents were born, and with great difficulty they took their cultural habits with them to Australia in 1938. Foreigners were searching for new lands in an English-speaking country, but they were not always welcomed. At first their traditions clashed with the locals, but their struggle won out as soon as their children became part of the foreign landscape.

I moved on to America to find myself, away from all the influences that didn't speak to me. It's interesting how we always end up where we started. Without having thought about it before, I had come full circle with my ancestral past. And that's when changes take place within.

Reflecting on the day's events on my way back to Istanbul, I wished my parents were alive to share my revelations: the spiritual places I had encountered and the influences of those that came before me. They both loved to travel, so within my heart I carried them on my journeys. I could hear them, speak to them, and their presence always brought me a feeling of being protected.

The next day I prepared to visit the great church of Hagia Sophia, built during the reign of Byzantine Emperor Justinian the Great (527–565). My driver arrived at my hotel with the filthiest car I had ever seen. I was embarrassed and peeved. "You're introducing me to your country in that?" He was a nervous young Turk effusive in his apologies. He promised to return as soon as possible with a better car. I hate hiccups on the road, but what would a foreign trip be without them? I waited patiently, keeping in mind that I was going to a magnificent church today to encounter new visions.

Within fifteen minutes he was back with a new Mercedes. I was pleased, but the Greek in me kept thinking, *There is something not kosher here.* Right away I thanked him and asked if the price would change.

"No, no, no," he replied. "My uncle, a very generous man, is giving you his car, which costs five hundred dollars a day, for free. And he wants to meet you, to apologize before we go to Saint Sophia. Seriously, he is very upset, could you please help me?"

My guard went up, I was suspect, and then it hit me and I smiled and said, "Does your uncle have a shop filled with carpets and many pieces of porcelain?"

"Yes, how did you know?" he asked.

"Psychic." I replied. "A Greek and a Turk together? We don't want history to repeat itself."

He looked at me blankly. "Because we are family now, our history is behind us," I responded.

Along the way I told him of my heritage, that our ancestors came from the same country. Maybe there was a Muslim mixed in there with a Christian. He laughed. This pleased him and so I was willing to go along with the game and meet with Uncle

George, just for the experience. Besides, coming from an ancestry of merchants, I'm always happy to sharpen my tools.

It was a beautiful shop, where salespeople smiled and shook my hand because they were fans of *Mission: Impossible*. They wanted to take photos together, but the young Turk was anxious to get me to his uncle's office upstairs where he was waiting patiently.

As I walked up the stairs I stopped to admire the beautiful blue and white porcelain that was on display. Uncle George was waiting at the top of the stairs and embraced me like a long-lost relative. I played along as a beautiful woman entered the space with a tray of desserts and Turkish coffee. The seduction began. The woman was all legs, displaying them through two slits on the side of her skirt. Every time she crossed her legs to purposely expose them, the uncle's smile reflected his approval. I'm sure that would disappear quickly if there were no desired outcome. But it did have its effect, and temptation was in the air. Lucky me.

Uncle George had already been on the Internet and got a quick grip on my history. "I love Greeks and, who knows, we could be related," he shouted out, enthusiastically.

He had seen photos of my house on the Internet and he loved the art, but the only thing missing, he said, were beautiful carpets to complement the collection. He went on with his soliloquy as merchant rug salesmen do. I had to finally interrupt, "Maybe it's because rugs live on a floor and I walk over them."

"Oh, but wait, I have such treasures to share with you." He snapped his fingers, bringing on the next show. Within seconds four men appeared with rugs hanging over their shoulders.

"But I am not interested. I'm sorry, I don't have the room," fell on deaf ears.

The rugs kept coming, and so did the special prices. I decided to sit back and go along with the game.

The coffee and dessert were delicious and the seductress kept performing. Then finally the package came together. The beautiful vases I spotted on the way up, which they noted, were also thrown in the deal.

"Twenty-three thousand dollars for the lot," he said. "Listen, I give money to my village every month so they have bread. They are so poor, and it's my responsibility to take care of them, that's why I need to do business with you today."

What a touching story, I thought. Or was it part of his routine to seduce the potential client?

I sat calmly for a while, revealing nothing. George was getting a little frustrated that I wasn't responding. The seductress kept brushing her hand over my shoulder, reminding me that she could be part of the deal if I was smart. The rugs kept coming and the prices kept dropping, and my expression remained unreadable, just like a poker player. But inside I was laughing at all the "sincerity and love" being thrown my way, and at George who was now believing he was at the top of his game.

Without a word I quickly threw him when I put my shoes back on to depart. He desperately kept interrupting with new proposals, but for me the folly was over. Without flinching I went right up to Uncle George, shook his hand and said, "The only space I have left is the closets, and that's not a place to see art." I thanked him for his enormous hospitality and said I would think about his offer, but after prayers at Hagia Sophia. I had to remind myself that I was still in need of his car, and it was important to leave him with the illusion of hope.

The expression on his face revealed his disappointment, and I could see his mind swirling. I'm sure the free car was echoing in his head too. At this stage the game was costing him. I kissed the lady on both cheeks to be respectful and thanked her for the show. She was perplexed. When I walked down the stairs behind the young Turk with empty hands, the people who previously asked me for a photo now had their backs turned. I left without fanfare, a stark contrast to my arrival. But the Greek definitely won that round, riding in George's luxurious car for free.

First we went to the Hagia Sophia district and visited the Basilica Cistern, meaning "Sunken Palace," an underground water complex built during the reign of Emperor Justinian in the 6th century. It took 7,000 slaves to construct it. I left my driver in the car sulking while I ventured to the water complex alone. I could hear classical music moaning from its depths as I walked down, and I discovered a four-piece orchestra playing violins to a Chopin concerto. It certainly added to the atmosphere of this mysterious waterhole.

The lighting was magically displayed in many rich colors throughout the structure as I walked along the planks over the shallow water beneath me. There are hundreds of these cisterns in Turkey created to hold water during times of war. When I arrived at the other end I discovered a large head of Medusa carved upside down at the bottom of a column. The ripple of the water made her snaked hair come alive with great effect. Nearby lay another, engraved with raised pictures of a hen's eye and slanted with tears. I read that the tears were a tribute to the hundreds of slaves who died during the construction in ancient times. It made it all the more effective with the music echoing in the background. As I continued through, I counted 336 columns of a marble forest that supported the ceiling of this enormous

The cisterns. (Author's Collection)

Hagia Sofia. (Author's Collection)

9,800-square-meter complex. It originally held 80,000 cubic meters of water. What an atmosphere it created. *Good place for a murder*, I thought.

It was now on to Hagia Sophia, the Church of Holy Wisdom. This former Byzantine church was later converted into an Ottoman mosque, but today it is a museum. The architects of the church were Isidore and Anthemius, professors of geometry at the University of Constantinople. They were entrusted with the construction of the Cathedral and supervised one hundred master builders and ten thousand laborers. The finest materials were brought to Constantinople from around the known world to create this masterpiece. Their work was a technical triumph and a great contribution to the heritage of mankind. It took almost six years to complete from 532–537 AD, and during the opening ceremony Emperor Justinian entered the cathedral and cried with pride. Remembering the Temple in Jerusalem he said, "Oh Solomon, I have surpassed thee."

Later earthquakes and invaders damaged the church, but after 1,500 years it still stands in all its glory as a magnificent monument of Byzantine Expressionism.

While crossing the street I could hear the young Turk arguing intensely over the phone. It was probably a battle with Uncle George over the failed encounter with the Greek upstart. I left him behind and concentrated on this universally acknowledged church.

Sophia's riches can be seen not in Istanbul but in the treasury of St. Mark's Basilica in Venice, stolen by Venetian looters in the 13th century. I proceeded up the stairwell to the higher gallery levels where the mostly restored icons are displayed. It was created that way so the Muslims did not have to confront the Christian imagery in the main chamber during prayer. Such stunning pieces of work, even with the damage done, cannot take away the power they still exude.

I walked around exploring the beauty of its setting, especially the splendid Apse Mosaic depicting the Virgin and child and the Deesis Mosaic of the triumphant and kingly Christ. Outside the window I could see the beautiful Blue Mosque, which was strongly influenced by the style of this church. Hagia Sophia remained a mosque until 1931, and reopened in 1935 as a museum by the Republic of Turkey. But now the crowd of tourists came pouring in and it was time to go. The size of the crowds was overwhelming and the sounds deafening. I no longer felt I was on holy ground.

Still, with its rose-colored walls and its beautifully designed dome, the Basilica is an impressive work of architecture — and how amazing that it still stands after so many earthquakes. It was the shape of its octagonal structure that helped balance and preserve it through the centuries. When I walked through its many halls I could not believe the grandiosity of the dome at its center, over one hundred feet wide and fifty-five feet high. The only distraction was the enormous calligraphic roundels hanging on the piers. They were added to the church, eight in all, in the middle of the 19th century, bearing the names of Allah, Mohammed and the first four Caliphs. I found them a distraction, because they didn't belong to the original expression of this sacred place, the first masterpiece of Byzantine architecture. The ancient Christians would have wept over this ugly imposition. When we add our beliefs to a different culture, we intrude upon its initial vision and deny its rightful expression, but it's called history, no matter how ugly the intrusion.

It was in 1453 that the Ottoman Turks, under the Sultan Mehmed II, conquered Constantinople, the "New Rome." He ordered the cathedral converted into his Imperial Mosque that lasted for over five hundred years. All things pertaining to Christianity, icons, bells and the altar were removed and the mosaics plastered over due to the Islamic prohibition of iconic imagery. But today some of its original art has been uncovered and the golden mosaics of yesteryear are shining brightly again.

Outside the cathedral the young Turk was waiting for me, but this time there was a smile on his face. Intuitively I thought he had another plan up his sleeve. The bidding game was not over. I asked him to take me back to my hotel. When we arrived I thanked him for his generosity, but he kept walking along with me into the foyer when his cell phone rang. No surprise, it was his Uncle George and he needed to speak with me urgently.

The young Turk smiled and handed me his phone. "Do you remember the village I spoke to you about earlier that I support? Well, I had forgotten and the payment is due tomorrow. I will make you a deal that could kill me, but it's for charity," the uncle blurted out.

"No, don't say that, but how sweet of you to call," I replied.

Now that he had my attention I listened passively to his aria. He went on about the rug and vases, and he was willing to bring the price down to ten thousand dollars due to the emergency that had arisen.

"Only ten thousand dollars?" I said with disbelief.

The nephew who was listening put his hand across his mouth in disbelief, "Oh, my God, he has never done that before, and he must really like you."

I put my hand across my heart and whispered, "I am touched."

I told Uncle George that I would be interested at that price. Enthusiastically he said he would pick me up at noon tomorrow and after completing the deal he would personally take me to lunch. I pretended to be moved, while he was probably rubbing his hands in delight. Beaming, the young Turk left to receive congratulations from his relatives.

The concierge who was listening to our conversation called me over to his desk. "But Mr. Penghlis, have you forgotten that you're leaving in the morning for Cappadocia?"

"Yes," I said smiling.

"But you won't be here when they come to pick you up."

"I know, that's the idea."

He laughed his head off. "You are a killer."

"True, my merchant ancestry would've been proud," I replied.

I went up to my room to pack without any guilt. Happily, I left in the early morning to catch my plane to a new adventure, an hour's flight outside of Istanbul. The travel agents dropped me off at the airport, but unceremoniously did not escort me in as they usually do. I was really tired and I had forgotten to get my schedule from the agents. When I looked up at the boards I saw five planes leaving for Cappadocia.

But which flight was mine? I eventually stood in each of the five lines to get a boarding pass. By this time I was afraid I was going to miss my flight. I had visions that I had to go back to Istanbul and discover Uncle George, distressed, waving his sword at me. Fortunately the hour flight to Cappadocia went smoothly, and when I arrived my guide was there waiting for me. He turned out to be a very charming and informative man with a good grasp of the history of Cappadocia.

We traveled for an hour until out of nowhere I viewed one of the most amazing physical countryside landscapes I'd ever seen. It was formed millions of years ago by volcanic forces, creating a soft porous rock called tuff.

Through erosion, it created the most wonderful "fairy chimneys" and other remarkable formations, giving Cappadocia its unique and unusual physicality. It was in the 1st century AD that Christians began inhabiting these geological marvels and, oh my, did they leave their mark. Due to the soft nature of the rock, they were able to create houses and churches. Carving through the stone, they created furniture within the rock and painted magnificent images of Byzantine icons inside the church's walls. They stood like sculptures in a museum, providing its inhabitants with a fairy-tale image. Although in reality it was a serious life held together by faith.

I went crazy taking photographs of the air balloons above me, floating effortlessly across nature's magical kingdom. I marveled at it all. I would have loved to have

Inside Hagia Sophia, Istanbul. (Author's Collection)

flown over all of this, and seen it from God's eye, but having survived two balloon crashes in Egypt, I was not so ambitious that day. Besides, I was under contract with NBC and I had to be responsible — money more than life, you know.

I went back into the houses and churches to get a feeling of the ancient life, noting that the frescoes on the church walls revealed the importance of their faith and salvation in this tormented land. It was still a breathtaking sight, conquered by many aggressive civilizations through its 2,000-year existence. I wondered why all of the structures were empty of human life? Where had they disappeared? Were they conquered and dispersed?

Cappadocia. (Author's Collection)

My guide remarked that these spellbinding rocks, which had sheltered the persecuted for so many centuries, were just as dangerous to live in as fighting their worst enemy. I was shocked to hear that for generations the villagers had suffered painful deaths, known throughout the region as the "Agony of Karain." It was diagnosed as a cancer epidemic, caused by the pale yellow rock that inhabits the region. The entire population of Karain and its nearby villages were evacuated and it was declared a disaster area.

"So what are we doing here?" I said half-jokingly.

"One day is not going to hurt you," said my guide. "But let's move on to another village with a different, but equally evocative landscape."

Cappadocia has many small villages and every one with a different face. Within twenty minutes we arrived at our next destination. Here the formations resembled a sea of giant penises. Obviously they did not bother the Christians. Some of them stood sixty feet high, with soaring entrances to protect them from the enemy. I climbed up the stairs and walked into this fantasy-looking house and watched through my mind's eye thinking about how simply these people lived.

I found the spaces they created for burial most unusual because they were inside the outer edge of the house walls. They actually kept the family together in this claustrophobic space. But to them it was home, and certainly no house taxes had to be paid. As I stood at the opening, observing what the neighborhood of the time must have been like, I laughed at the image of a bunch of chatty chimneys, screaming across at each other with the latest gossip.

Next my guide suggested we explore another environment lying on the other side of the hill. We climbed up to the sandy top where I was surprised to discover hundreds of small grape vines packed with fruit on the flatlands below. The birds migrated from the farmlands and dropped the grape seeds onto the sandy soil; the result is a life surviving wildly on its own. The texture of the steep slope was a bleached, sandy terrain, hardened by the elements with not a tree in sight. I was tempted to taste those wild grapes growing in the land of my ancestors.

My guide instructed me to descend slowly as the hill was slippery. I carefully began walking down the unwieldy slope, and my feet struggled to get a firm grip on the ground. Momentum had me walking faster and faster and I was losing control. Now I was running. Halfway down, I caught a glimpse of a large bush, hanging at the edge. I spun my body quickly into the air and landed in the bush full of large thorns. I let out a loud cry as the needles penetrated my back. My guide carefully walked over and pulled me off. He took my arm and we reached the bottom safely. He repeatedly apologized for the incident because he felt it was his responsibility to keep me out of harm's way. I assured him I was fine until I took off my shirt and the pain began. It was intense.

He slowly removed the piercing thorns from my back, wiped away the blood with my handkerchief, and rubbed alcohol over the wounds. This guide knew his business, always keeping his medicine kit with him for emergencies.

Covering up my discomfort I said, "It's Mother Turkey welcoming a Greek into her arms."

I laughed away the pain with my little act of bravado, thinking if I had gone flying onto my face, as I could have, I might have lost the love of my producers back at the studio in Burbank where they would have had to alter the story to compensate for my accident. When you work on a soap opera, death is a wonderful way of punishing the actor. After all, I had been resurrected six times, and I was not in the mood to die again.

I am grateful for the respective deaths and resurrections of my characters because they afforded me the opportunity to take my journeys and receive the reward of a great education. It also filled me with such strength and knowledge that I was able to incorporate these experiences into my roles. That was the secret to my survival in this competitive world — to fill myself with life and get paid for expressing it.

After this latest escapade I spent the rest of the afternoon sitting in a shaded café in a village called Avalos, taking in the worn faces of men with huge mustaches and colorful costumes retelling stories of their ancestry and how they fought the enemy in battle. They somehow brought me into their conversation by sending me a tray of sweets as a gesture of friendship. I was touched by their generosity, realizing that this was once an enemy of my ancestors. You would never have known it. We shared our history and spoke of the great warriors of Greece and Turkey in the War of Independence at the turn of the 19th century. It finally brought the withdrawal of the Ottomans from Greece, after four hundred years of Turkish occupation. By not arguing and just enjoying our differences, I could feel their passion, reflected through the way they sang and played their instruments.

In the end we took photos of each other, kissed respectably and knew that something had changed within us. Somehow the pain of the past lessened a little, the trust increased a little more. In this neck of the woods life was not in a hurry. And speaking of trust, I found another carpet shop across the street. Remembering my previous experience, and not wanting to repeat it, I entered the premises without fanfare. Standing in front of me was the exact size and design of carpet that Uncle George had tried to sell me for $23,000. When the salesman approached I asked, "Just out of curiosity, how much is that rug?"

Charmingly he responded, "Just 5,000 U.S. dollars, would you be interested? I could work a deal with you?"

Here are some simple rules I've learned if you're inclined to make large purchases during travel:

No is a very handy word to apply when in doubt.

Leave the building when they're expecting a sale, giving you the upper hand and returning on your terms and your price.

Really low-ball them, and if they have too many excuses, leave. And watch the chase begin.

Cappadocia, Turkey. (Author's Collection)

The final stage of the trip was going into the underground cities where the Christians lived as a place to hide and protect themselves during wars or when battling the elements. The only city I visited was nine stories deep. When I entered, the temperature dropped thirty degrees, a great relief from the heat. With narrow halls opening to the empty living quarters and tapered steps leading to its unbelievable depths, I walked down four floors until I began to feel claustrophobic. There were bright neon lights to show the way through, but I could hear what sounded like hundreds of German tourists coming down toward me. I went back through the complex and squeezed my way through the tourists going in the opposite direction. The air was so stagnant that I felt it difficult to breathe, but eventually I found my way out. As I fought to catch my breath, my guide burst into laughter when he realized we both had the same phobia.

Now it was time to get back to the airport and say my goodbye to my wonderful guide. He graciously waited and made sure I got off safely to Istanbul. That's when I tipped especially well for good services.

It was nearly midnight when I arrived back to my hotel. The same agents who had taken me to the airport picked me up, and I brought up how they had abandoned me without my flight information when they had dropped me off. They responded with no apology, just disinterest. When we arrived at the hotel and they opened my door, I stepped out of the van without tipping them. They shouted at my back in Turkish, and from their tone they were none too pleased.

"In America that's how we handle people who take their clients for granted, no tip," I calmly explained.

As I entered my hotel, they swore at me again. I went straight to the concierge who had recommended this company and reported their behavior. He apologized and in traditional fashion, swore he would "kill them."

"No, teach them," I said. "Because without tourism a country's economy falters, and you see this happening now in the Middle East." He agreed.

For me, there still remains a great mystery to Turkey. As I tried to investigate the nature of this ancient culture I realized that some things seen and experienced are never completely explained. I traveled to illuminate what's within through the connections I had made with my own heritage, from Istanbul to Gallipoli and Cappadocia, and through the sources of myths and the tales of becoming.

For thousands of years Turkey was a melting pot of many civilizations — from the Hittites to the Greeks, Romans and Asians, all contributing to this veiled society waiting to be exposed. The Armenian massacre, the illegal invasion of Northern Cyprus where they still remain today, and the brutality Turks imposed on the Greeks for four hundred years all influence my impressions. Turkey has received a great deal of attention as a result of its unsuccessful bid to join the European Union. But the leaders of Europe have indicated that before Turkey can join, it must improve its human rights record. It's been the subject of much controversy and international condemnation. Between 1998 and 2008 the European Court of human rights made more than 1,500 judgments against Turkey for violations on human life, particularly the torture of people who speak out against the State. When more than sixty journalists had been imprisoned, the U.S. State Department issued a statement that it had "broad concerns about trends involving intimidation of journalists."

Turkey became a NATO member and a valued ally to Europe and the United States during the Cold War because of its strategic location between Europe and Asia, yet little attention was paid to their poor human rights record.

I finally came to the end of this particular journey. When I returned to the United States and walked back through my own front door, I thought of my old adage "By coming full circle, a change in thyself will have transpired." I wondered what changes had taken place? I felt that by consciously going through the history of my ancestors I could clearly see a map now, imprinted by my family's footsteps.

It was an acceptance of the broad strokes they made by struggling and overcoming their identity, their Christianity in a Muslim world.

Walking the path of my ancestors has enabled me to acknowledge and embrace all of the history that had finally become part of my being. Having gone through it, and feeling wealthy because of it, I could move forward now and begin to trust the unknown before me. The lesson was this: "It's okay to look at your past, just don't stare."

View of the Bosporus, Istanbul. (Author's Collection)

Hatshepsut and the Valley of the Kings

Above Hatshepsut's Temple at Deir El Bahri in Luxor, Egypt. (Photo: Jack Betts)

It was dawn when my archaeologist guide, Mansour, and I began to climb the eroded cliffs of Deir El Bahri in Luxor, Egypt, situated 2,300 feet above the desert floor. After a couple of rigorous hours we reached the top of this arid landscape where we viewed the east and west banks of the Nile. That light that shined upon this civilization for thousands of years was awakening once more.

To the ancient Egyptians the sun rising in the east represented new beginnings demonstrated by the temples of Karnak and Luxor, while the west side, where the sun set on the Valley of the Kings and Queens' burial sites, symbolized death. As we continued along the ridge where so few, if any, tourists were now allowed, I was struck by that vision.

From high above, Hatshepsut's temple was on my right side and the Valley of the Kings on my left. As we sat taking in the remains of this phenomenal history, Mansour began to narrate the terrible tragedy that took place in front of this great temple in the early morning of November 17, 1997. Six Palestine terrorists arrived in Luxor joining a large group of tourists on their way to visit Hatshepsut's remarkable godlike structure. This mortuary temple is one of Egypt's greatest icons, and yet so little security was found protecting it. The terrorists blended in with the tourists and proceeded to slowly climb the steps leading up to the three-tiered temple. What followed was one of the most horrific attacks in Egyptian history. Throughout the complex, sixty-eight tourists were mutilated with machetes, blasted with bullets and stuffed with propaganda pamphlets right into their wounds. The murderers had left a note inside one of the victims praising Islam. It was signed "The Brigade of Devastation and Destruction." Five policemen were also killed. More security arrived and a battle ensued.

Desperate to escape, the terrorists began climbing the rugged terrain behind the temple and hid in the caves. The assassins ran out of ammunition and then smeared their faces with chemicals in order to destroy their identities. Seeing no way out because the military was closing in, the terrorists committed suicide. Their "ideal" in all of this was that a massive terrorist attack would devastate the Egyptian economy and provoke the government of Mubarak into repression. And so it did. For many years after, this massacre brought tourism to a halt.

Standing at the edge of the ridge, I was now facing those same caves where that final battle took place. I thought how cynical it was that they chose to ignite this modern-day massacre in front of a 3,500-year-old mortuary temple. Politics, will they ever evolve? I found it creepy, and I kept looking around as if they were still there.

But where was Hatshepsut's mummy? When British archaeologist Howard Carter discovered her tomb named KV20 at the beginning of the 20th century, he found it empty. He then proceeded to find another tomb called KV60. Without any knowledge of whose tomb it was, he climbed down four hundred feet, and found it full of bats. It was slippery and the most uncomfortable tomb he had ever walked through. Two female mummies were found. One was a wet nurse, and the other was torn apart and discarded out of its coffin. The riddle had begun. Carter took out the wet nurse, donated her remains to the museum in Cairo, and left the other mummy as he found it. He closed the tomb and regarded it as insignificant.

When we passed the caves I came across something unusual at this level, a tomb bolted and hidden away from the Valley of the Kings. I asked Mansour what was discovered at the bottom and he said it is where Hatshepsut was found.

As in step with previous experiences of coincidentally finding what I was looking for, I had found myself in front of the very tomb I was seeking. Before he could elaborate further, a loud scream in Arabic was heard from below the edge. It was a group of secret police running up the cliff's face, shouting, "What the hell are you doing here?" Since Mansour was a registered archaeologist, he animatedly explained our situation. We calmly took out our documents, knowing all too well the dangers of being interrogated by these unpredictable forces. They screamed back at him for not having a document giving him permission to be there. I understood their concern because of previous attacks, and so I kept quiet so as not to arouse any further scrutiny. They double-checked my documents, wrote my name down and left as quickly as they had arrived. We took a deep breath, but had to leave.

Finding our way down, the heat began to rise. At 9 a.m. it was already 115 degrees. I kept wondering, "Who was this mysterious and powerful Pharaoh who had taken charge of Egypt and morphed herself as a man?" She brought great prosperity and stability to Egypt and controlled the country for twenty-one years, and yet there is no record of how she met her end. Behind that crowning ridge in the Valley of the Kings lies her empty tomb, KV20. There was more to discover.

Finally on ground level I began to climb the steps to her temple, ignoring the oppressive heat. It seemed different to me this time around. Because of the massacre story, I found myself checking every space we passed through, even though the police presence was strongly visible. I still didn't feel safe, as the atmosphere remains so unpredictable here because of all the fanaticism. Today, the human element is gone, and what we're left with is the uncertainty of the times.

When I reached the top tier of her temple I found myself facing a bolted door that led to a secret tunnel ending at her empty tomb in the Valley of the Kings. At three hundred feet long, difficult and dangerous to access, it is the longest known tunnel in Egypt. Senenmut, her architect, was the steward of her possessions but lacked noble origins. Due to this they had to meet secretly through the tunnel and into her tomb. It was not until this century that the archaeologist Zahi Hawass discovered they were lovers.

He found hieroglyphics hidden in a small corner behind the door in Senenmut's tomb, revealing their great love for each other. It was indeed a well-kept secret. Love was obviously forbidden due to Hatshepsut's position. When Hatshepsut died around 1458 BC, her co-regent and ultimate successor, Thutmose III, had most of the images of her as Pharaoh systematically chiseled off temples, monuments and obelisks, negating all memory of her reign. It was to prevent her journey into the afterlife. He did this so that when he took reign all evidence of her existence as the king was eliminated and the male line would continue again without interruption. Even Hatshepsut's only daughter disappeared under the new Pharaoh's rule.

One of Egypt's greatest Pharaohs, Thutmose III became the Napoleon of his time, and a warrior without peer.

It was not until 1989 that archaeologist Donald Ryan rediscovered the tomb. Finding the disheveled remains, a wooden coffin was made for this nameless woman. Even after she had died it appeared she had been brutally attacked. With new technology available, a scan was performed on her and the wet nurse as well as two other unidentified women. Still no clear solution. Hawass, who was the head of antiquities in Egypt at the time, spoke one evening on how he remembered finding a small wooden box carrying Hatshepsut's seal and internal organs locked in a nameless tomb. It also contained the remains of many Pharaohs hidden from looters during ancient times. Now the puzzle of her life was slowly evolving.

He immediately ordered the scanning of the box and its contents. What it revealed was a molar tooth discarded in the intestines. They examined the X-rays of the four women's skulls to see if there was a missing tooth.

Lo and behold, a missing molar was discovered in the X-rayed skull of the disheveled woman. It was a perfect fit, and so Hatshepsut's identity was revealed at last. But why was her body so violated? She was an astonishing woman who lived as Pharaoh and brought great prosperity and stability to Egypt. Her mortuary temple symbolized the beauty of that power. Obviously she had her enemies.

I left Hatshepsut's temple feeling melancholy, having walked through her ruins and studied this Pharaoh King's most unusual life. The beautiful and powerful statues that guarded her temple and the obvious desecration of her images are held within the most unique structure for its time. It was so contemporary in its execution that it was hard to believe it was over 3,000 years old.

My journey was not yet over. I was compelled to witness her recently revealed mummy, which was now in the Cairo Museum. My travels are really like a mystery novel, searching for clues that bring about revelations.

I entered the Cairo Museum and headed straight to the Mummy Room where Pharaohs of Egypt's Golden Age were housed. The first King I spotted was Ramses II and, boy, did he give Egypt a heritage, including fifty-two sons. He died in his nineties and outlived most of them.

As I looked past him I caught a glimpse of Hatshepsut and I just wanted to go and pick her up and hold her. I felt like I knew her, having explored and read about her mysterious life. I walked around to the other side and watched her mummy intensely. She was different from all the others as she was covered in beige linen right up to her chin, not allowing us to see her as she was found, disheveled and discarded.

Covered in dignity she had been reunited at long last with her extended family of fellow New Kingdom Pharaohs, a world from which she had been separated for over 3,500 years. But her eye sockets were packed with black resin, her nostrils plugged with rolls of cloth and her head was completely without hair. She had no jewelry, no finger coverings or golden sandals, and yet she looked more beautiful than anything, simple, like someone happy to be home after such a harried journey.

By trying to destroy her memory and violate her spirit, Thutmose III made her even more famous. The discovery of monuments and hieroglyphs built during her reign, covered through centuries of wind-blown sand, gave us a clearer picture of how she lived. On one of her monuments resonates her charming insecurity as Pharaoh: "My heart turns this way and that, as I think what people will say. Those who see my monuments in years to come, who shall speak of what I have done?" That answer was easy. The world of archaeology certainly has spoken.

I looked at her surroundings, at the rest of the leaders of the ancient world, and remembered how Anwar Sadat, Egypt's assassinated leader, took offense with this display of royal remains. Being a spiritual man he thought it disrespectful for the public to view them. They were removed and put away secretly for twenty years. It wasn't until Hosni Mubarak, Egypt's last "Pharaoh," took Egypt's reign after Sadat's death and had them all reinstated back into the museum. Can you imagine, being in one room with so many of the great Pharaohs of Egypt's golden past, protected in a room with all your relatives? I was elated by what surrounded me. It was overwhelming.

My journey complete, I knew I would be back. I decided my next exploration would be the route that the Holy Family took in Egypt after escaping Herod. His edict had stated that "every male child be put to death" after he found out that a new king was born. For three and half years they roamed the Nile until Herod's death. Today, monasteries, churches and sacred wells have been acknowledged and established by the many miracles that have taken place. I will be expecting my own and why not, isn't life a miracle?

On top of Deir El Bahri in Luxor. (Author's Collection)

The Great Escape

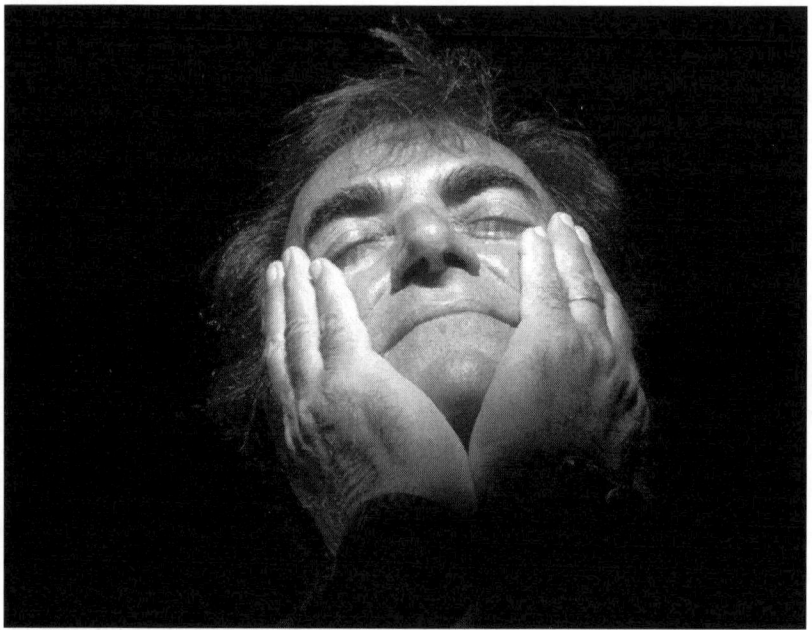

Inside Gabal al-Tayr Church, Egypt. (Photo: Jack Betts)

> Arise and take the young child and his mother, and flee into Egypt,
> And be thou there until I bring thee word.
> For Herod will seek the Christ child and destroy him.
> —Gospel of Matthew, 2:13–15

The flight of the Holy Family was understood to be a fulfillment of biblical prophecy, "knowledge that comes before its time." Egypt was a place of refuge for iconic figures like Abraham, Joseph, Moses and now the Holy Family.

I was intrigued with their sojourn ever since I read in the year 2000 that Pope Paul defined their route as hallowed sites and was now considered an important part of Christian legacy. Up and down the Nile they hid for almost four years, escaping Herod's secret police. Their presence in Egypt created the Coptic religion and Egyptian Christianity was born.

But how did this flight begin? Astrologists and scientists have placed it between 8 and 4 BC. In the city of Saba, north of Persia, three priests, Balthazar, Melchior and Caspar (dream interpreters for the King's Court), were struck by an unusual occurrence in the universe — the eclipse of Jupiter and the Moon. They interpreted this as a sign that something extraordinary was to take place in the location of Judea. A new king was to be born, whose presence would change the world. It would take them three months to prepare for this pilgrimage. Together they placed in three boxes gold (divinity), frankincense (holiness), and myrrh (to anoint the dead — sign of the physician) and departed for their journey 750 miles away from Babylon. It was to become one of the most famous pilgrimages of all time.

As they entered Judea on their way to Bethlehem, the Magi crossed paths with Herod the Great (37 to 4 BC) and proclaimed the birth of a new king. He became terrified, knowing the Jews were eagerly awaiting their Messiah. Had he already arrived? His fear of being dethroned by a new king and answering to Rome enhanced his paranoia. In his devious manner Herod asked the Wise Men on their return to inform him of the location of this newborn so he could worship him as well. They agreed to respect his wishes.

The prophecy came through when they met with the Holy Family and presented the Christ with their valuable gifts. The Wise Men, fulfilled and enlightened by their pilgrimage, began their voyage back to Persia. But one of the Magi had a dream. A professional dream interpreter, he saw "the danger of being arrested and Herod's attempt to assassinate the new Messiah." For their own protection they decided on a different path. Upon hearing this, Herod grew insane. Feeling threatened, he presented an edict calling for "the massacre of all newborn males." Hundreds were slaughtered.

And so here I was in Cairo in July 2010, hoping for a miracle. Pilgrims for centuries have flocked here in large numbers to pray at these sacred sites, to ask for miraculous healings or to simply connect for a sensory experience of their faith that brings the mysterious within reach. Mothers bring their children because they believe that a baptism at a pilgrimage site will bring extra blessings for their child, and for them it is about the direct connection between the believer and creator. And because of their faith, much has been answered to these believers. But when a miracle takes place that is psychological it doesn't sustain, whereas a true miracle like the boy in the wheelchair who got up and walked for the first time at a church in Samanud sustains forever. For centuries miracles have taken place and the Christian church has noted these divine blessings. But in this scientific world, unless it is proven it simply boils down to faith, and that I was willing to have.

Summer is typically not tourist season, so that's my favorite time to travel to the region. It also gives me greater bargaining power when dealing with Arab businessmen. I love playing this little game in the Middle East, getting them to the point of exasperation and their final (final, final) offer. Just when they think they've got me on the hook for a purchase, I walk away. The trick to winning at bargaining is knowing when to move on, and those are the times they come chasing. And lest you think I'm devious, rest easy knowing they expect this. It's their version of a game of chess or poker. It's serious business with a dose of folly and wit. And when they lose, by letting something go significantly lower than they'd like, it only makes them hungrier for another opportunity to be the victor.

The downturn is the heat, which at times can be overpowering. Your mind is not always clear when temperatures become that intense. Men of that region are in their element and use it to their advantage. They quickly size you up and go for the kill. I had to learn that the hard way through experience, and that way it remains.

Across the street from me was a hotel with a travel agency where a solitary, bedecked and bejeweled woman held court. I was tempted to ask for a date, just to see her reaction. Women, serious and untrusting in a man's world, grab one of the few opportunities they have of holding on to power. And apparently this job was her power. We discussed day trips and journeys, and I respectfully engaged until the fees were presented. I believed that this was where the bargaining would begin, as the prices seemed overly inflated. Especially for summertime when tourism is lean. But there was no bargaining with her. It was a one-offer deal. So I stood, thanked her politely and left. No bargaining, no chasing, not even an on-the-spot deal, popular with her male counterparts. Nonplussed, she returned to her phone, jewels flashing. She didn't get a client but she maintained what she considered to be the upper hand, and that was more than enough for her.

Earlier that morning in my meditation I had asked for guidance about my search, through a sign I would recognize. Exiting the agency, three men were standing by a desk. As soon as they saw me they quickly approached. At first I thought they were secret police until they asked, "Could we be of any help? We drive to any place in Egypt, and offer good prices." They were hungry and anxious. I asked them for a map of their country and they spread it across the desk. My first question was "What kind of cars are available?" They showed me photos of their vehicles, and I ended up choosing a tinted-glass jeep.

We strategically mapped out the best route to take, following in the Holy Family's footsteps. I told them I would return that evening after giving them a chance to think about a price that would satisfy us both. So later that day the agents presented the fee for the journey. The number brought a smile to my face. They smiled back, breaking any barrier between us. No negotiation was necessary. They were as reasonable as their fee, and my prayers were answered.

The next morning we would begin my sacred journey — Muslim and Christian together exploring places that can be seen, experienced, but never fully explained. That is where the imagination can soar.

In the world of Christianity you have to have faith for the experiences to have meaning. And when you return through the door you started from, something about you will have changed. And that's what my journeys are about: stepping into the unknown and filling a void with things that help me better understand the reasons why I am here.

At dawn I meditated on one of my favorite prayers to get my mind clear, so I would begin this journey in harmony. It's also how I try to look at life in my missions of discovery:

Salutations to dawn.
Look forward to this day, for it is life.
For in this brief course, the bliss of learning,
The glory of action, the joy of knowledge
For yesterday is only a dream and tomorrow is only a vision;
But today well lived, makes every day a vision of happiness
And every tomorrow a dream of hope.
Look forward then to this day.

Hani, my driver and guide, picked me up from my hotel at 6 a.m. with food and wine to celebrate our beginnings and discoveries together on what would be my ninth trip. He was a sweet human — he reminded me of a big bear. He saw me as a big brother who had arrived at his doorstep with blessings from Allah. Hani was respectful and never presumptuous. He seemed happy that he had work in this scarce environment, to put food on his family's table and to have a client who seemingly knew more about his country than he did.

On this morning our first holy stop was El Ashmunein, 250 kilometers south of Cairo. I didn't know what to expect, except that it was famous for its thriving port on the Nile when visited by the Holy Family. The Greeks — who built the tall Corinthian pillars that still stand proudly today as well as the massive underground basilica that was built in the 5th century — called it Hermopolis.

With my guide Hani in front of Farouk's Palace. (Author's Collection)

Through that maze of traffic and pollution we eventually got out of Cairo and were in an expansive desert. Thank God the roads there are decent. The only issue holding up traffic is the occasional Bedouin and his herd drifting across the highway with all the time in the world. We stopped numerous times for coffee, asking authorities for directions to Hermopolis.

Despite the heat, the starkness of the desert landscape was hypnotic. There were miles and miles of nothing but sand. I wondered if any ancient ruins lay beneath it as only thirty percent of Egypt's history has been discovered. Hani and I sang along to Western music to keep us entertained, until we arrived at our first village four hours later.

The residents are always curious and amused by foreign dress, the perennial shorts and designer clothes festooned with expensive toys while the villagers here are all covered up in their simple "Galabeyas." The average wage here is so small that ways of making money through foreigners are aggressively played. They cheered our arrival, but there was nothing we wanted or needed to buy. We got out of the car and gave the children some candy, which delighted them. We quickly drove off toward the Nile River, with the children running after us, shouting, "Bakshis, bakshis, money, money!" Fifteen minutes later the Corinthian columns appeared in the distance, standing majestically since ancient times.

When we arrived I was a bit surprised how small the place looked. I even walked and jumped into a hole where a posted sign read "Basilica." The earth had fallen in over the years, and the entrance was covered. This was a sacred place? Hermopolis was far from being the most zealously excavated site of Egypt, and the ruins here were to a large extent pulverized. I was not impressed except for the columns that were barely standing. There was a small sign made of tin, that had now rusted, hidden among overgrown weeds, stating "the Holy Family was here."

Really? It was something to see that this ruin, once a thriving center for the Cult of Thoth, the god of wisdom, healing and writing, and where the myth of Jesus walking through and the trees bowing in his presence, had all but disappeared.

No miracle here, I thought. And when a journey starts like this you begin to have doubts about what's waiting for you next. It felt empty, disbanded. But I reminded myself about my purpose here, as a voice kept whispering into my mind, *remember, faith*.

I sat on a broken column for a while taking it all in. I wondered what it was like for the Holy Family during those ancient times, under those conditions — the fear of being chased by Herod's soldiers, the amount of time it took to travel by donkey and on foot in this blistering heat. It was simply their faith. So what did I have to complain about? At least I had the luxury of riding in a comfortable car trying to imagine their path and the struggles they went through to save the Christ child, while hiding in caves and meeting the occasional generosity of villagers along the way. I had no fears; all I was doing was conducting, hardly a pilgrim. It was time for my next destination, Gabal al-Tayr, the Mount of the Birds, one of Christendom's most sacred spaces.

With Ashmunayn behind us, we drove for the next two hours in search of a village by the Nile where the Church of the Virgin Mary was situated. The villagers gave us many directions, all ending up nowhere. But then one man who spoke some English reminded us that the Nile in ancient times had been flooded but now it had receded for about half a mile inland. If we followed this particular road to its end we would find the church situated at the top of a cliff. Finally we saw it above us and climbed the 166 steps to the courtyard. No one around except children playing ball, we knocked on the church door. When it opened, there stood a Coptic Christian elder in humble dress, smiling and inviting us in. He proudly showed us around the enormous columned church while my driver, Hani, translated for me.

The church and its entire structure were carved out of a single giant rock, and that's what made it so amazing. The thick columns were fascinating to touch, blackened by the hands of thousands of pilgrims; again I felt I was part of this church for having walked its path. I put my arms around the pillars and embraced them, trying to sense the vibration of those who came before me. Later the keeper of the church told us the stories behind the icons that hung on its walls, many depicting the Holy Family's flight into Egypt.

Behind the altar was a locked door which is opened only by Father Matta during times of ceremony. I donated some money to the church, and I was rewarded with a chance to walk inside and explore its contents. In the middle of the room was a large piece of red velvet covering an object the size of a head. Was this something sacred? I'd read that when the Holy Family came to this spot, a piece of rock had fallen off the cliff and would have killed them had Jesus not lifted his hand and protected his family. His little hand left an imprint on the rock, and that is why the area is also called "the mountain of the palm." Is that what this was? I asked the keeper but he would not answer. He went off to reward me with something made by the church. My curiosity soared. As soon as he left I put my hand underneath the cloth to feel, and as I've said before, I have to touch to know it's real. It was something solid, covered also in plastic and revealed only by Father Matta on very special occasions. I felt a little guilty when the keeper walked back in and handed me some beautiful handmade candles. I had come so far searching for God.

Did it matter that I could not see the hidden treasure that lay inside the church's private quarters? I did touch it, and maybe that alone was a blessing. All I know is that during the summer months, thousands of pilgrims come here searching for answers, just as I did. And the answer for that search is revealed when we are ready. I thanked the keeper and went outside toward the cliff's face, overlooking the lush Nile Valley.

A sign posted on an outside wall by the Egyptian Antiquities says that Helena, the mother of Constantine, the first Christian emperor, founded the church in 328 AD. What a coincidence, I thought. She was the first pilgrim who visited Jerusalem, searching for relics of the Holy Land, and she eventually found the Cross of Jesus' crucifixion. She also discovered the Magi's remains in their tomb in northern Persia. The Cross was split into many parts and sent to churches of the known Christian world. Even the Crusaders of the late 12th century led their armies with part of the Cross — as their symbol of God's blessing. This powerful force led them to conquer Jerusalem in 1192 AD. Helena took the Magi's remains and other religious relics back to Constantinople. They eventually disappeared during the Crusades under the

German crusader Barbarossa, and the skeletal remains of the Three Wise Men ended up in a magnificent cathedral in Cologne, Germany, where they are still interred today.

Suddenly many Christian children bombarded me with their hands open, screaming for money. Hani started reprimanding them, but children always have a special place in my heart, especially the poor ones. They always remind me of the many struggles in my youth. I told Hani to have them earn bakshis (money) by telling me a story about the church I didn't know.

One young volunteer said confidently, "It was a cave where the Holy Family stayed as they fled upriver from the pursuing soldiers, and the church was built over it in the 4th century. But beneath the church lies a Pharaonic temple that has never been excavated." When he proudly finished I applauded and rewarded them all; their smiles were worth it.

Money in Egypt has a different fabric. The children looked at it as a blessing from a stranger. They hugged us, a long goodbye, and I knew we were on track. It was time to move forward to my next destination, the Church of the Holy Virgin at Musturud, known for the cave where the Holy Family hid from their enemies, as well as the blessed well that was created by Mary. It was a two- to three-hour journey south of Cairo.

On the way we stopped at numerous villages, all painted bright colors, their floors covered in dirt. The only form of transport was the donkey and the cart, and on the Nile an occasional felucca would sail by on the smooth waters. We saw children who looked like paintings — so beautiful, shy and untrusting with foreigners, they would hide behind their mothers or their animals. I saw a young boy pulling at a water buffalo along the water's edge, and I thought it would make a great photograph. We stopped the car immediately so I could capture the moment, and as I took the picture the boy screamed at the top of his lungs, letting go of the huge buffalo, and ran for his life. The animal, now loose and dangerous, went off on its own. It was total chaos. The men ran after the buffalo as I tried to explain to the families that I only wanted to take a picture. Hani helped quiet them down. Hani translated to me that the boy had seen men kidnapping children on television and he thought I was out to get him. It really upset me that I caused that much fear in a child. So I went over slowly to apologize and handed him some money, which he then handed to his father. What more could I do? We all took a deep breath, smiled and moved on.

We arrived at Musturud in time to hear the muezzin calling out to prayer. The distorted grating sound reminded me of the Middle East, mysterious and surrounded by veiled architecture. The Coptic church had an arched entrance filled with mosaics

Stepping into the light at Gabal al-Tayr in Egypt. (Photo: Jack Betts)

of the Holy Family. I entered the church while Hani went next door to his mosque where their holy ritual blasted through microphones.

Inside the Christian church the sermon was a quiet ceremony. What a contrast between two religions. I purchased some candles and went downstairs to the cave for which the church is famous. Against its main wall was a mosaic of the Madonna in prayer with hundreds of candles burning beneath in her honor. I sat there quietly taking it all in, the essence of that space lived in by the Holy Family. At these times where fear permeates the world, a story that rekindles faith encourages all of us beyond the gloom and doom.

A young boy came down and went straight into prayer, oblivious of me being there. His palms placed upwards, he dove into a fast prayer then turned and smiled at me. He did his cross and flew back up the stairs. This happened continuously with children getting out of school. When it all got quiet again I lit a candle and gave thanks for this pilgrimage and again asked for guidance and clarity along the way.

I came out of my prayer and I could hear the commotion of children playing, laughing and drinking water and washing themselves out of a well.

Below the church in the cave where the Holy Family hid. Boy praying in Musturud. (Author's Collection)

It was hot and my turn to cool down, so I got a little crazy, once again splashing as much holy water over me as I could. And drank as much as I could. I wanted Holy flowing through me, and no matter what reservations I had, the sounds of a Coptic liturgy filled my being. Those rituals always made me feel closer to God — that direct connection when a sound touches your core and your doubts disappear into the light. Above the well was a printed sign revealing the history of this sacred space. The spring still runs after 2,000 years. The Virgin Mary used to bathe and wash the clothes of Jesus here, and by connecting to that source I found my revelation. As a sage once told me, "Let it flow through you, not from you." When it flows from you it comes from ego, and through you it comes from a higher source.

I met Hani outside. He looked very disappointed. He had gone into the mosque to first wash his feet and arms to be clean for his God. He took off his watch to bathe and forgot to put it back on. During prayer he remembered the watch, and he went back to the washroom after prayer but it was gone. It was a watch that his father had given him as a young man and now it was lost.

"They stole it during prayer. What is the matter with people, they are not listening? So much for God," he said sadly.

I tried to comfort him, but to no avail. This watch was his treasure, a jewel of his youth. I know how much it meant that it had come from his poor father. He said it was time to go back to the hotel and rest up for the next day, so we moved on. For a brief moment I wanted to buy him a new watch and rescue the situation, but it was not my responsibility. There are so many struggles and so much poverty in this country that you can't save everyone. Giving him work was rewarding enough and he was grateful.

We returned to Cairo, passing hundreds of multiple apartment buildings constructed with little to no heart. The city is ugly in style and color and engulfed in heavy smog. With a history overflowing with such ancient wonders I was surprised and disappointed by their architectural choices. And if they ever had an earthquake, these buildings would collapse like a house of cards. I then realized that the ancients were not part of the culture that existed today. It came down to this — Cairo was a dying and overpopulated city with many riches yet to be found. Their government cared little for its people while they lived in their expensive fortresses, pocketing the country's riches. Isn't history repeating itself? Always.

The only thing that would change this system would be a revolution, but fear permeates this city because of the brutal secret police controlling its people with an iron fist. They are easy to spot in their plain clothes, their eyes always looking to arrest.

I've had encounters with them and I know firsthand that they can be quite threatening.

The next morning Hani picked me up for the next stage of our journey to Samanud, a few hours outside of Cairo. We arrived to find a noisy city where locals sold their wares in the marketplace while women and children sat on dirty sidewalks calling out their specials of the day. Hundreds of fish and animal parts hung in doorways; hundreds of flies swarmed over the hanging meat with no refrigeration. I stood there repulsed, thinking, *How could they eat that?* Obviously health inspectors were not an issue here.

I was surprised when a butcher's son approached me with a plea. "Take me away with you to America, I don't want to die here," he whispered.

Hani pulled me away. "You can't save everyone," he said.

I turned back. I looked into the stranger's eyes and he was crying. I sympathized with this poorly dressed young man who appeared to be in his early twenties, his hands already worn because of his hard life. Hani's voice echoed and we moved on. It was hard to believe that this was once an important city with magnificent architecture where many massacres occurred during Pharaonic and Ptolemaic times.

Within a few minutes I came upon the Church of Apa Anub. Prominently standing outside in its courtyard was a large heavy granite bowl encased in Lucite that was used by the Virgin Mary to grind grain to make bread for the family. A few feet away stood a well, blessed by Jesus. And for those reasons both became symbols of blessings for the church of Christian faith. I put my hand through a cut circle large enough to touch the sacred bowl and placed my written prayer inside it, a prayer for its people.

Objects like this in the Coptic world resonate for all of us. Its history made you feel fortunate and blessed for being there. I could hear the faint sounds of a Coptic sermon coming from inside the church. I walked in and it was packed with Christians on a Saturday morning. They turned and looked at me, this foreign intruder, with great curiosity, but to me it was a place of God and I felt safe. I couldn't understand the sermon but that's not always a bad thing. Your imagination expands through the sounds and the expressions on people's faces. I stood there for an hour studying them, and all my mystery dissolved when the crowd began smiling at me.

Apa Anub is dedicated to a twelve-year-old boy, along with the Virgin, who refused to bow to the Roman idols. Roman soldiers massacred eight thousand people, mainly women and children. Most pilgrims come on July 31, when the martyrdom of Anub is commemorated, and parents bring their children hoping for extra blessings. Many miracles have taken place here and there are three booklets recording the miracles in recent years.

One famous one is the boy who after a few pilgrimages kept asking for the intercession of the saint, finally struggled out of his wheelchair and walked. The church keeps the chair in an enclosed window as evidence of that miracle, along with many other objects. Even though these miracles seem unbelievable to Western ears, the difference between Coptic and Western thinking is between faith and rationalism.

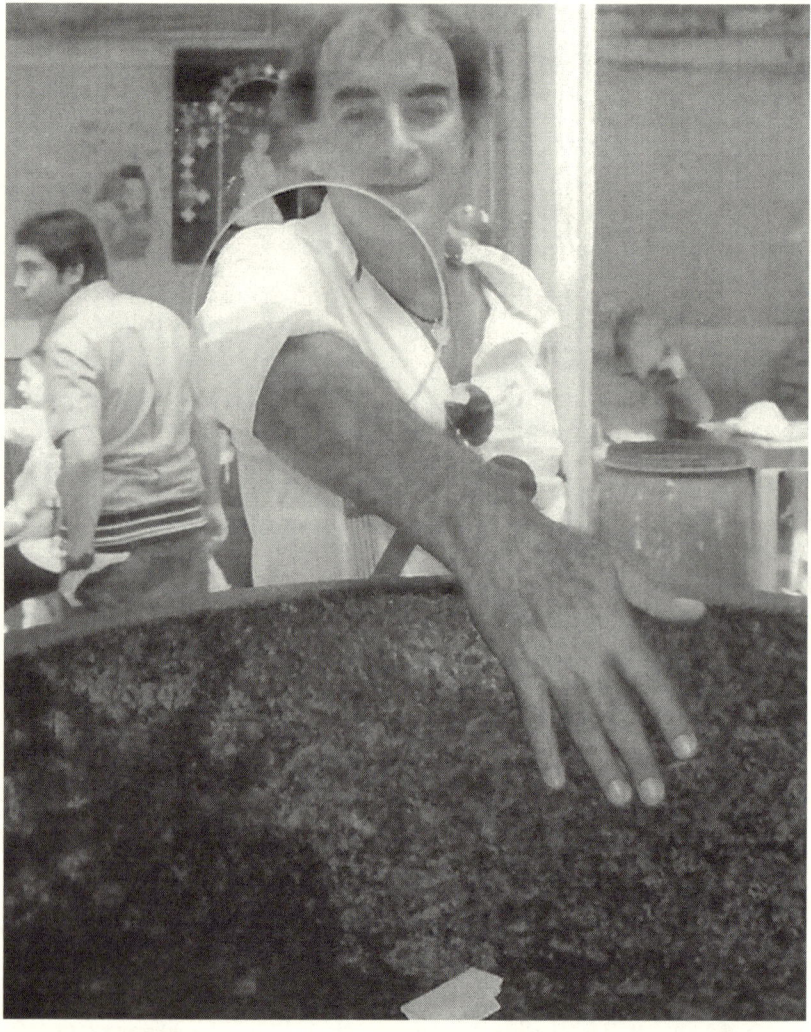

The Virgin Mary Miracle Bowl. (Photo: Jack Betts)

I thought back to the beginning of my story when the Magi had paid homage to the Christ-child, and the gifts that helped support them during their flight in Egypt. But only myrrh is mentioned at the beginning and the end of Jesus' life, where this spice was used to embalm his body with linen wrappings, the burial customs of the Jews.

When the Wise Men discovered the birth of Christ in the astrology chart, did they also see his death? Was that why the myrrh was presented as one of their gifts, for his embalming? Knowledgeable as they were of the Universe, I believed they did. When Herod died an angel appeared in a dream to Joseph in Egypt and said, "Get up and take the child and his mother and go to the land of Israel, for those who were seeking the child's life are dead." After three and a half years on the run, Joseph and his family returned to Israel and settled in a town called Nazareth. The prophecies would be fulfilled and he was to be called the Nazarene.

Now at the end of my search and after seeing how all these people lived, mostly in hardship, it made me reflect on my life now that I had traveled through these sacred places. What miracle was I hoping for? And then it struck me. I was already given one.

I had arrived in America with just two hundred dollars in my pocket and survived in this competitive world with as much freedom and success as any soul would need. I wasn't sitting in dirt somewhere begging for deliverance; no, I was sitting in the comfort of my home praying for miracles in Hollywood. But in that place God is always sleeping. It's a cutthroat business, greatly entertaining where often the only consistency is betrayal. Of course there are happy experiences when a breakthrough is made and a star gets an award or acclaim or the opportunity to do really good work, but it's the acquisition of money that dominates the scene. It's a fairy tale with a sting, and I've loved being there and surviving. It's been one of the best educations I've had in professionalism.

We returned to Cairo and I said goodbye to Hani. It was sad but what came together was a friendship with great respect for each other. We embraced and the big bear let me go.

Little did he know that four months later modern Egypt would be thrown into such disarray, and no one saw it coming. The people screamed from the bottom of their lungs so all the universe would know their suffering, and this time the world was paying attention.

Sign above the sacred bowl in Musturud. (Photo: Jack Betts)

The deposing of Mubarak would set such precedence for the rest of the Middle East, unseen in modern times. They were all handed a revolution, dictators were exposed, new powers reluctantly handed to its people, but a price was paid. Many died or were arrested fighting the military and secret police, those henchmen that constantly brutalized the powerless and the outspoken.

But in these times of scarcity, for challenging authority and putting their lives on the line, a miracle was handed to all the people: a freedom that most of them had never experienced in the thirty years of Mubarak's reign.

The youth in the streets brought an awakening, a spring and a revival, making history personal and changing the face of the Muslim world with no end in sight.

Discovering a Holy Site

The flight of the Holy Family out of Palestine was part of biblical prophecy. In the Gospel of Matthew the Lord appeared to Joseph in a dream and said to him, "Arise and take the young child and his mother and flee into Egypt and be thou there until I bring thee word; for Herod will seek the young child and destroy him." There are many monuments that document their escape throughout Egypt.

In the last few days of this particular journey, I had been reading about sacred spaces. Walking through old Cairo in an area called Babylon, I came across the old Greek Orthodox church of St. George. It was originally built in the 10th century but after a fire in 1904 resurrected again to its present structure. I walked up the steps into this place of worship, beautifully surrounded by ancient icons. I lit a candle for a blessing and as I have always believed, the simpler the words the better the prayer.

Suddenly I heard a monk calling me, "Are you Greek?"

"Yes," I said, smiling.

He put his vestments on and took me behind the altar and proceeded to bless me with incantations. After finishing his melodious ceremony, this simple man living under vows of poverty and chastity asked me to follow him.

He lifted an iron grate out from the floor and switched on the lights below. I proceeded to follow him down a spiral staircase. There at the bottom was a 1st-century Roman theatre.

One of the greatest moments I cherish in my journeys is discovering hidden sites where so much history is kept alive.

He then took me through a tunnel, and in the middle of it was a small room lit with candles, illuminating the icons around it.

"This is where the Holy Family stayed for three months while hiding from Herod's secret police," he explained. "This is the well blessed by the Virgin Mary, where her family drank from its sacred waters that are still flowing today."

I marveled that just three days ago I was reading about this and fate brought me to it. Another signpost? The right path? All I could think of was that I was standing on holy ground.

Before leaving he said, "Sit here as long as you like. Drink some water if you are thirsty, and when you have finished come back up to the church; I will be waiting for you."

After he left, I pulled up the bucket from the bottom of the well and not only drank from it, but splashed the holy water all over my face. It gave me a sense of connecting again to the ancient past. No matter how many people had passed this way, it couldn't help but make one feel that it had waited for you to arrive — and that I always believed.

Sitting on the floor of the alcove where Jesus, Mary and Joseph hid from Herod I felt I was in the presence of God. I wondered what it must have been like for them, their thoughts, their fears and the prayers the Virgin Mary had said to bless this well.

Before I climbed back up the stairs, I remembered again the poem by the Greek poet Constantine P. Cavafy called "Ithaca":

"When you travel to Ithaca, make sure that your journey is long, full of adventure, full of discoveries."

It is a poem about exploring the paths we take in life and conquering the fears that rise up before us. Somehow any fears of the unknown disappeared while sitting in this ancient theatre, reciting "Ithaca" in that small space where the ancients spoke. I felt embraced by an audience of Holy Spirits.

Back in the church, the monk was rolling handmade candles while blessing them at the same time. He handed them to me and said, "To light your way home." He walked me through the convent and outside the church, his arm around my shoulder like an old friend, sharing his insights and stories about this ecclesiastical life.

A shaman once told me that in another life I lived a life as a monk. Was this why I was singled out, through recognition of a previous existence? What I sensed as I walked out of the church grounds was that a shadow within me had been lifted, and I knew then I was not walking alone.

Inside the great church in Cairo. (Author's Collection)

Inside the basement of St. George's Church, Cairo. (Author's Collection)

The impressive great church interior. (Author's Collection)

Passage to Troy

As I've previously related, since childhood I've always been fascinated with ancient treasures and the heroes that discovered them. One of those heroes is Heinrich Schliemann, who in the 1860s became known as the "Father of Archaeology." His insights into Homer's work created a map that helped him discover an incredible treasure of gold. Across the Dardanelles and into Hissarlik of modern-day Turkey, he uncovered within a mound nine civilizations built on top of each other.

And so he began deciphering the riddle of which one of these nine civilizations was Troy. It had to be a burnt city because the Greeks (the Achaeans) had set fire to it during the Trojan War.

At enormous personal expense and with great difficulty he searched through the ruins below Mt. Ida where the ancient gods dwelled. Finally, in May 1873 with his wife Sophia beside him, Schliemann found the lost burnt city of *The Iliad* between levels six and seven. His discovery gave flesh to the mythical heroes of Homer and changed the face of history. A golden trove of necklaces (sixteen thousand pieces of gold) and other beautiful objects were found and donated to the Berlin Museum in the late 19th century. During World War II the treasure disappeared, believed to have been destroyed by the Allies during the bombing of Berlin.

Schliemann passed in 1891 outside a hotel in Naples. He died alone and his coffin was transported to Athens, where he was buried opposite the Aegean Sea so he could always see those famous black ships sailing to Troy.

In 1994, Schliemann's treasure surfaced in the basement of the Pushkin Museum in Moscow. Two curators, Akinsha and Koslov, found the war booty stolen in WWII inside the gallows of the museum. They brought it to the world's attention and ended one of archaeology's greatest mysteries. Greece, Germany and Turkey all laid claim to the prize but with no results. Russia was forced to exhibit it the following year, keeping Schliemann's discovery alive again, one hundred and fifty years after his death. The controversy still continues today.

I decided to follow Schliemann's footsteps by going to Athens and getting permission to access his diaries and documents in the Gennadius Library. Two weeks and 60,000 documents later, I felt as if I had entered his soul. Researching his personal letters from all walks of life in English and Greek, I felt transported to the 19th century. So many letters in front of me, I was tempted to steal a love letter to Sophia; it was a fleeting thought but satisfying nonetheless. That certainly would have made

Ruins of Troy. (Author's Collection)

Standing on the ruins of the real Troy. (Author's Collection)

me a hypocrite. I was sharing the room with a female archaeologist, and she looked up during that highly emotional moment.

"I felt the same when I read those letters. Very moving," she reflected.

I was sitting in the world of heroes, taking in the world created by Schliemann, when she extended an invitation for me to meet with the Minister of Culture.

When a meeting with the Minister of Culture of Greece took place that afternoon, I received permission to get a private viewing of Schliemann's mansion in Athens, a palace called The House of Troy where kings and dignitaries of the late 19th century had gathered. I walked through where they had dined and danced and imagined myself in their world, their stories, their Victorian manners, and the formalities that must have been exchanged.

I entered Schliemann's beautiful office upstairs, designed in bright colors and frescoes that imitated ancient Pompeii. I sat quietly in his personal space, taking in what I could about what he wrote in his books, letters and his theories of discovering a lost world. It was a great privilege. I felt blessed for what my world was offering.

I walked down that enormous stairway, where he must have come down greeting his guests with great arrogance when his fame had reached its peak. Later that year The House of Troy would be turned into the magnificent Numismatic Museum, continuing on with the world of the ancients. Schliemann would have been pleased.

The next morning, I visited his gravesite in the First Cemetery of Athens. There it stood, high up like a miniature mausoleum. Its reliefs described his conquests and on top his bust overlooked the mighty Aegean where the great Achaean warriors set sail with a thousand ships and conquered Troy. Staring at the bronzed door, where behind it laid Schliemann's remains, I dearly wanted to know how his body was interred. Like the myths he uncovered, it will be rediscovered again centuries from now, to be reinterpreted by different minds and greater technology. Later I spoke to the guards at the cemetery and they answered my question. Behind that door Schliemann was buried beneath the tomb, tiled over and above it, Sophia and her family's remains.

My next step was to see Troy for myself and explore the Homeric myths of the Great War and the love story of Helen and Paris that started it all. After a five-hour drive we came to the Dardanelles and crossed the waterway by ferry. An hour later we arrived at Çanakkale. From there a guide met me and on horseback we galloped across the Troad where the Trojan War took place. Like two ancient warriors we raced around and finally climbed up onto the mound overlooking Hissarlik. There it all was. Schliemann's World. His sacred ruins where he brought to life Homer's tales that carried him to glory. He was, in short, a born discoverer, and the discoverer, like the poet, is born, not made. Oh, those ghosts, and the battle sounds of long ago. If you listen hard enough that war is still raging.

We sat there at the edge of this battled site and opened a bottle of champagne to celebrate man's ability to go beyond himself and reach for his godlike being that inspires the passion within him. But what happened to the great love story of Helen and Paris that started this war? My guide looked at me sadly and shared that in Michael Wood's documentary on Troy, he says that, "In the archaeological archives, love leaves no trace."

Ballooning Over the Valley of the Kings

It was 5 a.m. in Luxor, Egypt when I boarded a small boat to cross the Nile River over to the West Bank. Luxor lies on the ancient site of Thebes, the capital of Egypt during its Golden Age. The Necropolis of Thebes contained some of the most incredible monuments in Egypt. The idea was to take a balloon ride over this entire splendor and experience it from God's point of view.

As we drove along in the early morning light we came across a pair of great statues standing ominously in the shadows called Colossi of Memnon. During an earthquake in ancient times parts of the faces and bodies had fallen off. What remained of these sixty-four-foot-tall statues was something so haunting, with expressions of such horror, only to enhance its mysterious presence. The original function of the Colossi was to stand guard at the entrance to Amenhotep III's memorial temple. It was created for the Pharaoh 3,400 years ago so he could be worshipped as a god both before and after his departure from Earth. In ancient times the entire area of his mausoleum collapsed and disappeared beneath the sandy landscape, destroyed by earthquakes and floods. But today huge excavations are taking place, revealing all that had been lost.

I stopped to take photos of these amazing relics only to be halted by guards protecting the finds. As soon as I offered money my actions were forgiven, though their expressions silently revealed that it was not enough. I ignored them and began taking more photos. Approaching the balloon we could see enormous flames pushing the hot air into the fabric. I was a little nervous, knowing there had been accidents with balloons before, and I jokingly thought I had not left a will or said any goodbyes.

Within fifteen minutes, I climbed on board along with twelve English tourists. The captain of our airship kept squeezing the lever, blowing the flame into the belly of the balloon. How it didn't catch fire was a miracle.

As we prepared for takeoff, the captain gave us directions and an explanation of landings for a smooth and effortless flight.

"Good morning, ladies and gentlemen. Before we take off, remember, stay in the boundaries of the basket. We normally experience three types of landings. The first is what we call the American landing: you come down hard. The second is the British landing: you come down hard but get dragged along anyway. The third is Arab: CALM."

And suddenly there we were, rising so fast and so effortlessly that I forgot my fears. I had never known such silence. In the distance the sun was lifting itself above the sand reflecting its morning light along the banks of the Nile.

There below us were the great monuments of Egypt, something the ancients could not have seen at this height. To my left were the sacred tombs of the Valley of the Kings. In this light it looked so mysterious, and yet I remember that in 1997 a group of terrorists jumped out of the surrounding cliffs and murdered sixty-eight tourists, stuffing pamphlets into their mutilated bodies. It brought Egyptian tourism to a halt for many years. It's very hard for me to shake that memory.

Up in the balloon the strong winds pushed us along. The Luxor and Karnak temples came into view like pillars of a stone forest. How grand was the scale of these images and their presentation to honor the gods in the afterlife.

As we descended, I spied a young girl running through the cane fields. She looked up and waved and smiled at us. I reached into my pocket and threw some paper money into the air. I will never forget the expression on her face. So excited, she scrambled around catching and collecting all of it through the cane fields. Her exuberant cry was so loud, as if she were receiving blessings from Allah.

As we were coming to the end of the journey, the balloon literally just missed some apartment buildings; it was so close we could almost touch them. We held our breath. One woman screamed, but our captain seemed to be enjoying himself, as if this were a perfectly normal occurrence. We came crashing down hard. But there was more to come. The balloon went up with great force and then crashed down again, dragging us along the cane fields that thankfully softened the otherwise harsh fall. I cried out, "British landing!" They were not amused. The English were frightened and unleashed their fury, screaming at the captain while I laughed it off as another experience.

Colossi of Memnon. (Author's Collection)

Ready to balloon in Luxor. (Photo: Jack Betts)

Among the new discoveries at the site of Amenhotep III. (Photo: Jack Betts)

Ballooning. (Author's Collection)

Ballooning over the East Bank of the Nile. (Author's Collection)

We were finally on the ground, the basket on its side. A donkey appeared out of nowhere and on its back sat a man in white with his feet almost touching the ground. "Hello," he said with a smile, as if lying sideways in a cane field was perfectly normal. In my mind I was looking up at Joseph with the Holy Family not too far behind.

A truckload of men arrived and began pushing the balloon upright. I looked at the captain and said, "I was hoping for an Arab landing, obviously, but the British won again, damn it!"

I didn't tip him, following in the British tradition. I loved it, drama and all. After all, what's a good ride without a bump? But a year later I read that English and German tourists had been involved in a balloon crash at Luxor airport as the strong winds took them off course where most of the tourists broke their arms and legs. Ballooning in Egypt came to a halt for the next two years. But the flying resumed after investors pressured the government, complaining there had been too much money invested in this highly popular and lucrative adventure. I'd fly the balloon again but only when the winds are calm during the early hours of dawn.

Colossi of Memnon, Luxor. (Author's Collection)

Dreaming of Casablanca

When I wagged school on occasion at the age of twelve, I got caught up with the revival of the 1942 film *Casablanca* in Sydney. In order to pay admission I had to comb the alley and search every nook and cranny where drunks slept the night away on cobblestone streets. I would collect their empty beer bottles and sell a sack full of them to the bottle yard with just enough coins to see a movie and buy some chocolate and popcorn. No one knew until I got caught a couple of years later forging a letter to my principal that I was too sick to attend school. I shrugged it off as character-building. Frankly, it was worth all the scolding I received, especially from my mum, because in that Victorian theatre I was free to dream in the dark where nobody could see me.

I fell in love with *Casablanca* and longed for the day when I could step into that city (although I knew the film was really shot on the Warner Bros. back lot). The characters lived through my mind my whole life.

It was a perfect story with iconic dialogue:

"Of all the gin joints in the world she had to walk into mine."

"We'll always have Paris."

"Here's looking at you, kid."

"I think this is the beginning of a great friendship."

Bogart and Bergman — there has never been a pairing like them. Years later, at a New York party, Ingrid Bergman asked me to dance. What a special memory — she was a part of my youth and now she was dancing in my arms laughing, just as I remembered her with Bogie.

Finally, some years later, my time came to journey to Morocco and led me to sit at the actual Rick's Bar in Casablanca.

My first leg of this trip took me to Milan, then on to Valencia in Spain and finally to Morocco for New Year's. It was the Christmas season and the streets were filled with people shopping for gifts. Milan was beautifully decorated, abounding in lights, and the sound of Christmas carols permeated through the city. I stood there in the square taking it all in with hundreds of pigeons in a feeding frenzy, swirling around me and landing on my open palms. It was surreal.

I walked through the arcade and bought some beautiful Venetian glasses for my friend Enrique Senis-Oliver in Spain. He was an extraordinary painter of Renaissance style. I'd known him from Los Angeles and spent a great deal of time watching him paint. Now he lives back in Valencia where he was born. His expressions are a thing of beauty, and I couldn't wait to see him and his new work.

I checked in at the Duomo Hotel. When I opened the windows in my room, I came face to face with the Duomo Cathedral. What an amazing work of Gothic architecture. The church took nearly six centuries to complete, starting in 1386 and evolving into a Renaissance masterwork that stands as the heart of Milan, with its spires reaching for the heavens.

What a view — the carvings and the steeples, no wonder it took so long. I was compelled to see the inside, the soul of the place. Through the massive cathedral doors I stepped into this enormous space, filled with the sounds of a Christmas Mass. The voices that echoed throughout gave me the rare chance of feeling innocent, but cheeky. Like it was a new beginning, and it was fun. Ah, the smell of candles, the icons of saints, people expressing their faith. I held on to those moments where all the elements connected and you feel incredibly alive. You know you are back on track when answers you've been searching for surface and you've once again awakened your inner core. As I walked around the immense structure, I discovered so many artworks I'd never seen. Some were heavy in their setting. It's that guilt thing that arrives when studying martyrs. Religion can have its downturn. And there were some very rococo images, quite bloody, that I could not connect with. Heavy Spanish influence, I would say.

I recalled that in 1875 Oscar Wilde, the British writer, sent a letter to his "mummy" that the cathedral was an awful failure. He also said, "Outside, the design was monstrous and inartistic and so many details stuck high up where no one could see them, however it's imposing and gigantic, a failure and too elaborate in its execution." So much for taste. I thought it remarkable. I only remained in Milan as a stopover. My schedule was tight, as I would stay with Enrique in Valencia for Christmas and Marrakech, Fez for New Year's, and finally, Casablanca. The journey to new cultures was always invigorating and in some regards challenging. The unknown plays a great part in the excitement, and there is always the energy of apprehension when stepping onto new soil.

I arrived in Valencia that afternoon with Enrique and his manager David embracing and welcoming me to Spain.

My arrival brought back a vivid memory from the last and only time I was in Spain. It was about a decade earlier and I was refused entry because my visa was not stamped on my passport. Their policy had changed a few weeks earlier because of an incident in Australia with Spanish tourists. Now I was persona non grata and the immigration official blurted out, "I don't give a fuck who you are. You will remain at the airport and in twelve hours catch a fight back to London and get a visa." There was no argument.

When I landed in London and asked the authorities why they did not catch the visa issue, one replied, "Give the gentleman a nice hot shower and a cup of tea so he can relax."

"That's it?" I responded.

To which the official said, "Yes, what else can we do?"

"Take responsibility," I replied. The man just stared.

"Well, you can take the tea and shove it up your ass," I cried with exhaustion. I was angry and I was frustrated.

Feeding pigeons in Milan. (Author's Collection)

He was not pleased. I was dumbfounded. I had been up for thirty hours and now another eleven to get back, let alone the expense, and all they offered for their mishap was tea. Anyhow, now in the present, and all that past melted away, sort of.

Enrique was so happy and I felt content for he always brought out the best in me. I just loved him for his essence. He lived to create. Life for him was driven by passion. I had not seen him in twenty years, yet it was like yesterday. But you always know that when relationships have great memories, and most of all trust, there are no adjustments to be made.

We arrived at Enrique's glorious apartment at the center of Valencia. It was previously a loft where beautiful art deco ceilings were uncovered. The walls were displayed with his exquisite art, and great French furniture in bold colors was situated in the rooms. Above all, the scent of paint floated through the air, evidence of an artist constantly at work, interpreting life as he saw it.

After all these years it was amazing to see so much growth in his work. We sat up till four in the morning outlining a commission of an icon of St. George. My mother had always hung a small one of the saint above my bed since I was a child. She believed he protected me from negative energies. Now I wanted a triptych, because in my environment in Hollywood you need a large one to fight those Machiavellian forces.

We decided on a canvas, four feet by four of St. George fighting his mythical dragon. As Enrique had never painted a religious work before, this new idea challenged his imagination. It took him three months, but not only did it double in size, the result was an inspiring execution of such fine detail that when it arrived at my home I hung it on the center wall of my eighteen-foot-high living room. It took six men to lift it. When an art dealer saw it, he offered me three times what I paid for it. I couldn't give it up, as it now became part of my history. I have four of his paintings and he was pleased that I was a collector of his work. For me, it was a reminder of things well done, and that always put a positive spin into the living energy of my house. He threw a wonderful dinner party showing off his friend to his guests who were from all walks of life.

The next few days were spent seeing the city. The new architecture was evolving with Europe's modern era.

These new structures affected me, like the Louvre's glass pyramid in Paris. It doesn't always work. Aesthetically beautiful, but for me it doesn't warm the eye; it's a clash of cultures. I loved the city's main cathedral with its Spanish molding dominating its façade. Inside I came across the mummified arm of John the Baptist in its caged display. Was it real? I was told it was. I found it hard to pray to an arm but found the relic fascinating and revolting at the same time. Besides, I thought his head was cut off and supposedly sitting in the great Umayyad Mosque in Damascus. Religious relics are abundant, and there are some that exist in triplicate, each claiming to be the real one. But it's the sacred myths of these pieces that illuminates and helps people's faith when in need, serving a higher purpose, and from the expression on the people's faces it succeeded.

My last day was spent watching the artist at work. What a process it was sharing ideas with the painter and watching them come to life. His training, just like an actor, is always in the process of becoming. I loved to interpret his paintings and he always embraced my insight. I told him that "Inside the depth of his work was a monk with

Christmas in Milan. (Author's Collection)

arousing thoughts." We had a good laugh. It was a fulfilling short stay and I was sad when I left him. It's at those times you realize how people who use their God-given talent wisely make a difference, and because you're sharing it, leave the better for it. I miss that energy, it's rare and hard to find.

For the next stage of the journey, I was to fly to Madrid and catch my plane for Morocco. As I was filling in time at the Madrid airport I was checking out the usual trinkets when suddenly my flight was announced. I felt somewhat distracted, having left my friend Enrique so quickly I had little time to think what was ahead of me. It was a long half-hour walk to my gate, cutting through crowds and the usual obstacles at these international airports. When I arrived to pass through immigration, I realized my folder with everything in it, including $5,000 and my passport, was missing. It was very upsetting and my head was spinning with all sorts of dramatic scenarios. I quickly retraced my steps. I only had an hour to catch the plane.

Enrique's *Fallen Angel*, hanging in my Los Angeles home. (Author's Collection)

The only place I used my folder was at the newspaper stall. I drove my trolley through large crowds, praying all the way and excusing myself like a mad driver from Cairo. It took twenty fast minutes to reach my destination, and now I was flying. How could I have been so careless? Breathless, I entered the newspaper shop. It was very crowded. My heart sank. I moved my way through, expecting nothing but a miracle. I stopped at the *International Tribune* pile and there sitting on top of it was my folder. I stood there, dumbfounded. I slowly picked it up, but there was no one to thank except God and the universe, which I did all the way back to my gate. When I opened it I realized nothing was missing. I chastised myself for creating such worry and angst, then stopped everything when I knew right away it was a signpost, to be present and aware where I was headed — to a country rich in heritage and shadows filled with clever merchants. I was finally on my way to Casablanca, feeling the excitement I felt all those years before as a young boy dreaming in the dark of exotic places. And of Bogie and Bergman, of course.

I arrived in Marrakech later that evening. All went well through immigration and customs, and I had prearranged for a hotel driver to meet me at the airport. That's always important, then you don't get hassled with unreliable or tricky drivers because sadly cons are always lurking. I had had to learn that the hard way in the Middle East, so I always reminded drivers that I'd been to their country many times and knew their history well. I took charge of that game. You have to.

I arrived at my hotel and went to bed early. The next morning the desert sun was shining through my window as I caught my first glimpse of Marrakech with its remarkable colors exploding through the light. I enjoyed a wonderful exotic breakfast while the concierge set up a driver and a guide. I began to explore the city, its narrow alleyways and its people with new eyes, having not been there before.

My first stop was the city's main square filled with a world of snake charmers, and the display of carpets filled the background with their earthy tones. The merchants were on the prowl, calling out to bring attention to their wares. My first encounter was at an artifact shop where the owner came right up to my face and whispered like a conspirator, "I love your face but I want your money."

I laughed. "You're getting neither," I said, and continued on my tour.

My next experience was buying two framed mirrors with camel bone and wood that was stained black. How vain of me, but you can always use a mirror.

The bargaining ensued until I made my final offer, a third of the initial price including air delivery. At first they said no and I walked away. My motto is this: If I meaning, each color revealing its secret language, and by embracing it, I reveled in this foreign atmosphere.

It was getting dark as the winter sun began disappearing below the hills. My guide took me back to the Jamal Palace, as it was time to prepare for New Year's Eve. That evening the hotel was throwing a big bash to celebrate the event. I put all my valuables in a safety deposit box and proceeded out of the hotel to take in the sunset, as this would be my last night in Fez before heading to Casablanca. I took time to speak to the guard who reminded me that danger was lurking always at this hour for tourists without a guide. We shared a cigarette, and as I walked away to the edge of the hotel ten young boys began to surround me. The guard watched from a distance. They began playing with their private parts to get my reaction. I knew that money was all they were after. The circle came closer and closer and I started feeling a little trapped. I began shouting at them. "Get home to your mothers." They continued to taunt, ignoring my demands.

"We give good massage up there in the forest, very cheap," they whispered.

No matter where I walked the circle never broke. I purposely left my valuables at the hotel because of my guide's warning. This time I was listening and this time I had enough. I started pushing them away and the guard finally came over, screaming in Arabic. Fearless, they were now reaching into my pockets. I began to laugh because there was nothing to steal, not even a watch. This threw them and that gave me the upper hand. The guard physically disbanded the group and escorted me back to the hotel. I felt like the character in Tennessee Williams' story *Suddenly Last Summer* where a man gets pulled apart and eaten by young men. I had passed through that danger physically unscathed but emotionally bruised. It was the character of the children that age, hustling for survival, that bothered me. What future did they have when starting out like this?

Half an hour later back in my hotel room I began getting ready for the New Year when I heard a bloodcurdling scream coming from the side of the hotel. I froze. It sounded like someone being killed. Two hours later at the celebration I would learn a tourist had been robbed and murdered. I sat at the dinner table with foreign guests, thinking how fortunate I was the guard had kept his eye on me.

I didn't like hugging and kissing people I didn't know at the midnight hour, so I excused myself and asked the concierge to send my dinner to my room. He didn't understand my desire to be alone and he kept reminding me, "But it's New Year." I tipped him and his tone changed. I needed to be quiet with all that had transpired since arriving in Morocco. The experience with the boys and tragedy of

Entrance to Mosque, Marrakech. (Author's Collection)

can live without it, I can walk away. They live to sell. They chased after me and they agreed to accept my offer. I was pleased. Air delivery is expensive.

I began taking photographs of vibrant colors with shadows falling across narrow streets, crossing paths with women completely covered in secret, men in black leading through the smoke, spices in heaps of such exotic colors, vocal merchants demanding attention, and cobras dancing to the sound of their master's flutes, all magnifying Marrakech as Morocco's most intoxicating city. Situated at the north of Africa, it's a gateway from East to West. It became a trading and resting place on the ancient caravan routes from Timbuktu. This city has barely paused. Dominating the country's landscape are the snow-capped Atlas Mountains, meaning "Land of God," and they are beautiful. They extend for 1,600 miles through Algeria and Tunisia. Religion is prominent, Muezzins are always calling to prayer, veiled windows through labyrinthine alleyways representing a hidden society. They see you but you don't see them. It all lends itself to an air of mystery that's unique to its identity. You try to unravel it by going through it on your own terms.

That is why I let my driver and guide go, which I found later to be a costly mistake. This time I felt I wanted to discover, rather than being guided. I had a good grasp of the country's history and wanted to experience it with fresh eyes. As I walked through the old Medina dating back to the 8th century, I crossed paths with donkeys carrying loads of produce, saw heads of goats displayed on large platters, heard the butcher crying out the shop's daily special, and watched the fabric dyers splash away their colors. I felt as if I had been transported into ancient times. The atmosphere was nothing short of a magic carpet ride. No machines, just human hands as the driving force.

When walking a new path that is this unique, your life expands at that moment, a shift takes place within you and you realize how fortunate you are to travel the world, full of eye-opening wonders.

I left the square and caught a cab back to the hotel. I had been walking around for hours and felt wonderfully fulfilled. As I entered the hotel, I realized that my camera and film were not in my hands. I rushed back out, but the cab was gone. All those beautiful photos disappeared in a split second. The concierge tried to locate them, but it was not to be. Once again on this same journey I was not paying attention. I had no philosophical answer for my mistake. Just a loss of photographic experiences I would not be able to duplicate. If I'd kept the guide it would not have happened. The images remained in my imagination, a sole consolation. Fortunately I always travel with two cameras in case an accident occurs. So the next day I continued on and hired a driver to take me to Fez, along the route of the majestic Atlas Mountains.

It was a beautiful drive to Fez, passing through that mountain range for hours. I sat back listening to George Delerue's film scores, adding extra emotion to the visual grandeur. These mountains God translated for us, to embrace, to take in and be inspired. My driver did not speak any English, which was perfect because then I could watch in silence. That's always a good thing because it allows the mind to rest and take in other aspects of the journey without interruption. I had a map with me and I could see what was coming up next. I felt like an explorer navigating unknown territory with my driver as a compass.

Later that afternoon we arrived in Fez, a city regarded as the jewel of the Arab civilization. It is Morocco's spiritual capital, carrying many secrets that do not reveal themselves easily. Secretive and shadowy, they need to be discovered carefully. It looked like the South Mediterranean, bustling with merchants, artisans, captivating sounds and fragrances spilling through its center.

I was staying at the Jamai Palace, which was transformed in 1930 into a luxury hotel that is situated high up on a hill. It had a beautiful entrance, brocaded in multiple-colored tile and old brass.

During the day it's a peaceful environment, but after 5 p.m. it becomes dangerous.

I hired a guide and went straight to the bazaar before it got dark. We traveled through a labyrinth of sloping hills to winding alleyways crammed full of merchants and donkeys. Medieval history reverberates through the tangled streets — the exotic sounds and visuals all contributing to the seduction of this incredible maze.

Fez's golden age was during the 14th century and presided over by the Maenad Sultans. I viewed their tombs from my balcony window, illuminating the hillside in the afternoon light. Like Marrakech, Fez is a hidden city with high windowless walls adorned with flowing Arabic script, impenetrable to the non-Muslim. They radiate with bold colors as the shadows of hooded men and veiled women pass by, reflecting the drama.

The colors portrayed radiated the importance of Morocco's culture with white as purity, blue for the sky, black for depth, yellow for wealth, and green for Islam. It gave the city more significance for I was able to translate the life around me through color. I finally arrived and had a delightful lunch at a restaurant where male dancers spun around for so long, I began to get dizzy.

My guide and I sat on the floor on large cushions while they served us maize and their famous pigeon pie. I loved eating with my hands, as was the custom, even though in the West we would frown upon it. I enjoyed sharing the experience with my guide who filled me in on the history of the place. Every design had a that late afternoon were not celebratory. I wanted to clear any negatives hovering around me by lighting a candle and doing a meditation. Even the danger had its purpose — "Wake up."

It's an interesting way to experience New Year's Eve, quietly without expectations. Because it's just a date, the extreme joyousness of people has always had a desperate undertone for me — like some miracle is about to happen, but never does. I wanted to start the trip to Casablanca with a clear head and not a hangover. This was the last leg of the journey, and my dream was about to be fulfilled. I loved Fez, faded but stately, and even though it's crumbling, it all adds to its myth and keeps its secrets alive. I didn't want to overanalyze as I always have found that when returning through the door where you started, answers will appear.

As we were driving toward Casablanca I felt like something was missing. In all my journeys to ancient cultures it was always walking through ruins, imagining the life that came before, that stimulated me the most. I noticed on the map that the ancient city of Volubilis was near the path to Casablanca. I asked my driver if we could stop there and explore it. He knew nothing about it, as was the case with most drivers, especially the Arabs, as their history didn't begin here till after the late 7th century, bringing in their language, customs and religion with them. Perhaps the lack of knowledge is because it clashes with their beliefs, as idolatry is forbidden. Still I think it's important to know who walked the path before you, and that was the Greeks and then the Romans. An hour later we arrived at the Roman city of Volubilis. I was back in my element.

The city was most dominant in the Roman period that ended in the late 3rd century AD. The only residents left are the storks that nest above the ruined columns. And there are plenty of them. It was almost comical, but it was life nonetheless. They are the best preserved ruins in North Africa, and in 1997 it was listed as a World Heritage site.

There weren't a lot of visitors and I felt at home here with no distractions, just sitting and being in harmony with the elements. It was a landscape rich in oil and grain, especially for the Romans. But the city's downfall was caused by earthquakes and the disassembling of structures to help build the nearby city of Meknes in the 18th century. As time was getting on, my driver signaled me that it was time to go. I wanted to reach Casablanca in the light. I got my ruins and that helped satisfy my passion for the old.

Entering the city edge of Casablanca were the grimy shantytowns of the rural poor, splashed across the country's landscape. It reminded me of Rio de Janeiro. The traffic jams, like in all Middle Eastern countries, were a mess. Mindless directions and lack of traffic laws with plenty of exhaust filling the air, leaving a metallic taste, I had a sunken feeling that my dream was to turn out to be a nightmare. I held my breath all the way to my hotel. I checked in and said goodbye to my driver. His last words in broken English were "Be careful."

I decided to take a walk and what I witnessed was one of the dirtiest cities I had ever seen. Its architecture was in need of a good wash. The name Casablanca means "white house," which did not apply under these conditions. I slowly entered the Souk and before I knew it at least twenty merchants were coming toward me with one thing on their mind: money. Every expression of charm filling their masked faces. Before I could take another step I was encircled. They came closer, touching, grabbing and shouting about their wares over each other. I couldn't breathe. I sensed danger and tried to leave but they held on: buy or else. I began laughing at their greed and that threw them. I remembered not to carry a wallet with me and showed them my empty pockets.

"Just sightseeing," I said.

Not a happy crowd I had attracted. I freed myself and kept on laughing, while their faces remained stern. Acting in the real world has its advantages. Having outplayed them, I left relieved.

It was time to sit at a café and observe Casablanca life from a public place. I had this eerie feeling that I needed to remain close to my hotel. As I was having Turkish coffee two men in their twenties sat at my table. They began a conversation and I just listened. They were rambling and I was wondering what they were after, when they asked, "When are you leaving?" My antenna went up. I remembered an experience in Rio when the same question was asked me, and I was warned that if that ever arose, recognize it as the beginning of a plan to scam you. It would take place the night before I left and that way I couldn't press charges.

I smiled and said, "Next week."

"But what day?" they kept probing.

"Tuesday evening," I lied back.

They went on about their lives and were clearly excited that I was from America — land of the rich. I played along with their game until they revealed their plan.

"You should join us Monday evening for a celebration with our friends to welcome you to Casablanca," they said.

"Will I leave happy?" I asked.

They were confused. I politely declined and their attitude changed. They persisted, and I continued to decline. Irked, they rose up with their mustaches curling. Out of the blue one of them placed a small ball of cellophane-wrapped marijuana on the table.

"For you, to keep you happy in Morocco, from your friends."

My blood curdled. They left and I quickly called over the waiter in case there were secret police watching. The waiter brought my bill and I pointed out the object that was left by the individuals who had sat there. He picked it up to smell it, and his expression changed. I never touched it and I told him to throw it away. It was the real deal. I looked around to see if anyone caught the incident, but there were so many people around I couldn't tell. I played it safe, but the incident bothered me because their intent made it creepy.

After ten minutes I'd had enough. I didn't feel comfortable, even though I had been in some tricky situations before; I listened to my instinct to go back to my hotel. I never left my room until two days later when I was exiting Morocco. I watched the rest of my dream through the glass of a hotel window. I never made any friends. That was a first.

I returned home through the door I left and began to think about my childhood dream. *Casablanca* was a movie I fell in love with, but when I visited, what I saw was life. Different, but the course I chose. The players were strictly business and their only motive was money, and how best to get it. Their sincerity had a different motive. There was no embrace, but like veiled windows that are characteristic of that society the myth proved true. I never got intimate enough to find out. Nor was I invited, just another foreigner passing through.

Morocco is a destination I would never make again. I never felt that about another country before. It just struck me that way. Whatever mystery I came across had left with the experiences I went through. They were thought-provoking, challenging, exciting, and disappointing when the evidence shot through film was lost. I still love the movie *Casablanca* as I realized we never saw much of the outer life in the film, just the intimacy of the characters.

I never found Rick's Bar, but what the hell, I can still dream, and besides, I'll always have Paris.

Christmas in Israel

In the summer of 2004, Palestinian gunmen held the Church of the Nativity in Bethlehem captive for thirty-nine days. Monks were trapped inside the Orthodox Church for the entire ordeal. The terrorists created a regime of fear. An Armenian monk and two Palestinians were killed. It was now Christmas Eve 2004 and the tension had died down. I was excited when I arrived at Tel Aviv airport. It was my first journey to Israel.

Leaving with my baggage I was quickly surrounded by four Mossad agents with badges flashing. I was flagged as a terrorist. Again. I smiled. They looked threatened and aggressively asked, "Are you carrying drugs?"

"What, on Christmas Eve?" I replied. Blank. I cut to the chase, having been through this before.

"I'm an actor, you probably recognize me from *Mission: Impossible*? I've been invited to do publicity here for the studio." Their faces dropped, their masks disappeared, and they apologized profusely through their embarrassment. It was lovely to see their human side. I enjoyed the drama.

My desire that evening was to find a guide to take me into Palestinian territory and pray at the spot where Christ was born. That evening outside my hotel in Jerusalem my guide was waiting and we quickly began the journey. Trusting the process and feeling I was on God's path, I went with him in a van across the border. Into a dark street twenty minutes later, another van was waiting.

They spoke to each other on the phone in their native Arabic language and began flashing their lights. I got into the next van, introduced myself, and by the time a third van appeared I felt I was being kidnapped. But this time a scholar showed up and put me at ease. Due to that tragic summer incident it was forbidden to go there without the proper connections.

We approached the square within ten minutes. In front of me was the Church of the Nativity where the Christ Child was born exactly 2004 years prior. Carols echoed through the ancient square. I remembered this was my parents' dream to be standing here at the center of the Christian world. They never did come because of the constant turmoil that exuded from this sacred space. I was in Palestinian territory on the West Bank and not a woman in sight.

Facing the church with my guide beside me, he explained the three entrances created through the ages. In ancient times a chariot could charge through. Over time the door had been diminished to a small opening where only one person at a time could enter. In front of it stood nine military soldiers blocking the entrance. No one was allowed in. Because of the earlier uprising it had become no longer a place of God but a fortress. The sacred place of prayer was shut. My guide explained my situation to them but they kept repeating, "It's closed." He apologized to me. "I'm not lucky," he kept saying. "I failed you." I told him I was not going to give up so easily. To have come all this way…I will call God in my own way.

He said he needed a drink.

"But aren't you a Muslim?" I questioned.

"I don't care," he said, betraying a great deal of frustration in his voice. "This place is like living in a box," he said. He explained that it's a reminder of their constant battle with the Israeli government. Two Scotches later my bravado rose up.

"Let's try again," I said.

"It's useless, they will threaten us again," he responded.

Losing my patience I replied, "It's Christmas. It's not supposed to happen this way."

With my guide Mohammad. (Author's Collection)

Determined, we ventured back and approached the guards. They stood defensively. The war was not over.

Suddenly the door opened and a Greek monk came out puffing on a cigarette. I studied him, thinking, God wasn't talking to him either.

He caught my eye and stared at me. "Are you Greek?" he asked.

"Yes," I replied.

"From *Mission: Impossible*? The masks?"

"Yes," I again answered.

He charged over and hugged me as only Greeks do, without apology.

"You gave me such pleasure while studying theology. What can I do for you?" he asked.

"It's Christmas Eve and I've wanted to go inside our Greek Orthodox Church since my childhood, and they won't let me in," I explained.

"Come with me," he responded. He put his arm around my shoulder and escorted me to the entrance.

The soldiers took a defensive stance with rifles threatening.

"Is this not a place of God? Then behave yourselves. This pilgrim has permission to enter."

God spoke, and the soldiers parted. As I bent down to go inside I turned to my guide, who couldn't believe the change of events.

"You said you were not lucky? Luck is when opportunity meets commitment," I told him.

Persistence won.

I followed the father in and sat at the place of Christ's birth: this sacred space where thousands have waited to take a glimpse of the most famous spot in Christian folklore. I had an hour to myself, uninterrupted. You can't help but be moved when touching the core of Christ's birth. It was no longer a postcard. I thought of my family and friends and the inner peace it touches within the depths of one's beliefs. I just sat reflecting all that had passed my way. Thanking the universe and feeling like a child again in its beginnings, my pilgrimage had evolved in a most sacred way.

Two years later while sitting in an Athens café, I watched two monks having a drink and a cigarette. After a few minutes one of the heavily bearded monks turned to my direction. "Do you remember me?" he asked.

"No, I'm sorry," I replied.

"I'm the priest who opened the door to you at the Church of the Nativity two years ago," he said.

What are the odds of that happening in this enormous world we live in? It was an emotional moment for me. We embraced each other like spiritual brothers. Another coincidence? Or simply recognizing the signposts of life and knowing you're on the right track — a reminder that trusting the process does lead to victory. These journeys are there for all of us, the difference lies in the way we see.

The historical birthplace of Christ. (Author's Collection)

Church of the Holy Sepulcher. (Author's Collection)

Lebanon

Ancient ruins at the Hippodrome, Tyre Lebanon. (Author's Collection)

I've always wanted to visit Beirut, a city regarded as the Paris of the Middle East and situated in the ancient Phoenician country of Lebanon bordering Syria and Israel. It's been ravaged by wars for centuries and most recently the Hezbollah war with Israel. This group of Lebanese militants has been supported by Syria and Iran, continuously threatening Israel's existence. The last major conflict with Israel took place in 2006, creating a war lasting thirty-four days. But the threat is always there, waiting to be ignited. And that was the atmosphere I was walking into.

If I had an Israeli stamp on my passport I would have been denied entry. The great thing about Israel is they only stamp a piece of paper when entering, and returning it when you exit so there is no evidence of your arrival. It all went smoothly through immigration except for the words that kept vibrating in my head when friends and colleagues in Los Angeles had offered me warnings: "Be careful, it's dangerous, you could get kidnapped, what if you don't come back?"

My first day of exploring Beirut was met with chaos. I thought Egyptian drivers were bad enough but Beirut takes the prize. I'm still getting over it. No lanes, no order, screw the red lights; it was a war within themselves, bleeding through their torment. Horns honking, people walking, abandoning the traffic, the motorcycles navigating themselves through the chaos, making me flinch every few minutes and thinking how the hell could they live this way? Could it be that the constant wars within Lebanon manifested itself into the lifestyle of its people today, chaos breeding chaos?

Michael, a Lebanese friend from Australia, promised to meet me at the Beirut airport, but he didn't show up. I waited for two hours. When I finally left for my hotel I was caught up in bumper-to-bumper traffic. What an entrance. I finally arrived and went straight to dinner as it was getting late. Michael finally appeared an hour later. His reason was, "I got lost in my own country, can you believe it?"

"How great," I said. "If you can't find the airport, how on Earth are you going to show me Lebanon?"

Through our dinner he passionately convinced me that he could, and besides it was a dream we had talked about for twenty years. But by the end of the first morning, after exploring the city, I needed a drink just to relax so that I could take a break from the rhythm of this chaotic place. Perhaps my friends were right. But a journeyman has to move forward through unfamiliar territory if he is to understand what drew him here in the first place. Michael couldn't stop laughing at my concerns, and so I eventually relaxed and joined him, reflecting on the amusing tales of our past.

The next day we were on our way to Tyre (Sur in Arabic), an ancient Crusades city south of Beirut and north of Israel. In the late 12th century the Christian leader Richard the Lionhearted and fellow crusader Conrad de Montferrat developed a rivalry over the kingdom of Jerusalem. Montferrat was one of the most successful commanders of the Crusades as he had taken the city of Tyre. He was now in a strategic position to open negotiations with Saladin, the Islamic leader, over Jerusalem. Conrad was killed in broad daylight on the streets of Tyre by a group of assassins known as the Hashashins, a group of terrorists that originated in Iran in the 9th century and who eventually migrated to Syria. Their ceremony consisted of taking hash before assassinating their victims in broad daylight. This ominous shadow was greatly feared as it struck from out of nowhere. Today it is believed they are the ancestors of Al-Qaeda.

Richard was a chief suspect of Conrad's murder because he wanted complete control of the Crusades while Saladin fought to keep Jerusalem under Islamic law. These rivals represented the symbols of the cross and the crescent. The leader of the assassins, Hassan bin Sabbah, was also a suspect. To this day Montferrat's murder remains unsolved.

Roman ruins in Tyre. (Author's Collection)

Three hours later I found myself in the heart of Hezbollah territory, driving through this city where all that history had taken place. I was excited, being surrounded by so much culture, from the time of Alexander the Great to the invasion of Islamic forces in the 7th century and on to the infamous Crusades. Now, in the 21st century, the Islamic military was strongly showing its presence. The previous day we were told that two Lebanese men were hung as spies for Israel. This ancient historical port was not exactly Shangri-la. The bullet-riddled buildings and the war-torn streets dominated the landscape. I stood there in disbelief watching the results of a modern battle, an end zone filled with people and machines. The only color was dirty beige.

After driving through the streets my friend Michael pulled into a gas station to ask directions to the ancient Roman ruins of Tyre. Out of nowhere a Hezbollah with a face like a bull stuck his face into mine threateningly and demanded: "Are you an Israeli spy?"

I said, "Grecia! Grecia!" not wanting to take out my passport, knowing that being an American here would create difficulties. He tried to stare me down, but I didn't flinch.

Michael, thank God, intervened with his broken Arabic, "No, no, he is a friend of Lebanon. Greek?"

He just kept staring, and finally dismissed me and told us to move on.

Lovely, I thought. I was at the edge, experiencing their drama. But it saddened me to see that many people's lives here have known only war and confrontation, a way of life imposed by other nations.

As we drove toward Tyre we observed numerous UN soldiers standing by their jeeps on the lookout for any trouble, and so we felt a little safer. An hour later we entered the Roman ruins of Tyre and found ourselves in the middle of the Hippodrome, where famous chariot races had been held. *Ben-Hur* came to mind. And so I slowly ran around the entire oval, listening to the cheers of the imagined mob. I was back in my youth and loving every second of it. I took a bow and collapsed in the heat. It was exhausting but exhilarating. The arches where the charioteers had entered were still standing. It was one of Rome's most popular sports where thousands cheered on their favorite heroes, where drivers used their skills and any other tactics, fair or unfair, to win. A magnificent ruin standing among the weeds, a shell of its former grandeur, but still there to remind us of its glorious past. My imagination soared.

After my imagined race we returned to Tyre, where I was shooting photos of the current landscape. Three security cars with tinted windows drove by. I started to photograph them, when I heard a loud "No!" I ignored it even though I knew that in the Middle East one is not allowed to photograph government buildings, police or military personnel. I pretended I was photographing the church in front of me. Two policemen accosted me and grabbed my camera. Thank God it was film and not a digital camera, so the evidence was not visible. They wanted to know why I was aiming my camera at the security cars. I humbly told them that I was photographing the Christian church, this place of God. A UN soldier, right out of James Bond, came into the argument. I explained everything to him and he convinced them that I was an innocent. Suspiciously, they handed back my camera. Sometimes I think the kid in me creates circumstances just to provoke and then find ways of getting out of them. It makes my journey a little more interesting although I wouldn't recommend it. I breathed a sigh of relief, as another obstacle was overcome.

As we moved on, our James Bond soldier (who oddly enough was from New Zealand) told us to be aware of our surroundings. Hungry to learn from his stories, we decided to invite him to a late lunch. We sat at a restaurant by the sea and listened to his tales of survival in this war-torn country. It was a world I found fascinating. He told us how an Israeli soldier kidnapped a number of years ago was an excuse by Hezbollah forces to begin a new war. Iran was delivering highly sophisticated weapons through Syria into southern Lebanon, helping Hezbollah create a new challenge to the Israeli dominance. Newly armed with more sophisticated weaponry they fought a new kind of war against their old enemy, and Israel realized that Hezbollah sitting at its border was now a force to be reckoned with. The Israeli soldier whose kidnapping started this last war was finally returned to his homeland. Israel pulled back and is now secretly preparing for another war. Will it ever end?

We asked the soldier for directions to Montferrat Castle, in particular the location where Conrad had been murdered in the 12th century. He warned us that the area was dangerous since Israel dropped hundreds of cluster bombs, ruining some of the ancient sites and riddling the place with over 100,000 mines. His expertise was in finding and disengaging them. What an incredibly dangerous life, I thought. And there I was, a few hours ago complaining about the traffic. It certainly places things in perspective.

It was an interesting day. I felt a little like a spy, the actor in me always attracting the unexpected and playing it as well as my cards would allow. We said our goodbyes and headed back to Beirut. It took three hours of intense driving. I never relaxed for a minute, always thinking the "enemy" could stop us at any moment. But then I thought about those soldiers and what they go through on a daily basis. I had nothing to hide, except being an American citizen. I was disappointed that I was unable to explore the area where the assassins struck. I enjoyed the Roman ruins, especially the Hippodrome where once upon a time thousands of spectators gathered to watch and cheer on their heroes. Their voices still echoed in my mind and all those ancient stones that I walked along evoked the wealth and beauty of the past; such moments of wonder raced through my mind. The green marble columns, the mosaic road, the magnificent arches I passed through and the coastline that I drove along was an extraordinary backdrop to this great Phoenician civilization.

Baalbek. (Author's Collection)

Two days later we began to climb the mountains on our way to the city of Baalbek, three hours north of Beirut but not far from the Syrian border. The terrain was absolutely spectacular especially during the winter when the whole area is covered in snow. It's Hezbollah territory again, so I knew I had to be aware of not attracting attention. But as usual I ended up doing just that. A jeep with three soldiers had their machine guns aimed right at us all the way up the mountain. Ah, the games of war that have plagued this whole area since the Crusades. Feeling uncomfortable with the present scenario, Michael decided to pull into the first possible stop at McDonald's, and let them drive past without incident. He always remained calm.

Finally we arrived in Baalbek at one in the afternoon. Not the ideal time, as the sun was burning down; it was 120 degrees, and no shade. I must have been a Bedouin in another life as I always ended up in a desert, this time as a hot-blooded Greek trying to be cool. Entering the ancient city, I thought, *What a glorious space*, filled by the largest Acropolis I had ever seen. I was blown away. Such enormous stones placed on top of others in perfect fit and alignment, built before the dawn of our most ancient cultures.

What minds could have erected them? Like the Pyramids of Egypt, they remain an enigma. In the main section of the forum a group of men were setting up a stage and lighting for a concert series; their first was to be Puccini's *La Traviata*. With crumbling ruins serving as a dramatic backdrop, it was the ideal location for such a glorious tragedy. During the Hellenistic period, the city was originally named Heliopolis, City of the Sun, by Alexander the Great. It is considered today as the most important archaeological site of Lebanon. But it was the Romans who eventually finished building this masterpiece. Some of its stone foundations weighed up to 1,000 tons. The final portion was built during Nero's reign in 65 AD. It was a true example of the power of the Roman Empire, expressing itself through its grandiose architecture. At the end of the 4th century AD the Roman Emperor Theodosius proclaimed Christianity as the official religion of the Roman world until the Arab invasion.

The destiny of the Baalbek Acropolis was sealed. The altars were destroyed, temples abandoned and dismantled so that the Christians could build a basilica over the courtyard. But in 636 AD, the Arabs conquered and transformed the Acropolis into an impenetrable citadel.

Standing in front of these ruins, interwoven with Christian and Islamic influences, I heard the voice of a fellow traveler say to me: "Can we at least sit for five minutes and take this all in — we may never cross this path again?"

So I did just that, thinking better to get it while you're here, instead of later when you're gone and memories are your only recall. I sat in the great Bacchus Temple and what a beautiful monster it was, imagining what great leaders, poets and artists had sat here as well, expressing themselves through their work.

Sadly, a lot of statue heads and carvings were destroyed during the Arab invasion due to the fact the Muslim religion did not recognize idol worship. Still, my senses stimulated, I recalled what the poet Cavafy expressed in his poem "Ithaca," "Don't hurry your journey at all, old as you've become, and with so many things to recall, you would have become as rich as your essence would have allowed." And what a visual and emotional feast I had.

I left a little apprehensive seeing the area still immersed with Hezbollah, a constant reminder of their ongoing conflict.

It was time to find treasures, not wars. I entered an antique shop and found some ancient coins made of silver and gold from the Greek and Roman periods. There went the bargaining again. It's as customary as having your daily coffee.

I counteroffered the merchant's deal by half. He hesitated. I reminded him of no tourists in his city and reluctantly he accepted. I was so excited by the coins that I kept bringing them out, hour after hour, feeling and looking at them again, thinking what hands and what exchanges had held these coins. They were now my treasures, legally bought, and I was taking them home.

My next journey was going to be a spiritual one, high up in the Lebanese mountains at a monastery called Mar Maroun, where the great Saint Mar Charbel's remains are interred. I only discovered his story when the hotel concierge remarked about his miracles.

In the Christian world of Lebanon this was their holy place. In the mountains above it all, lies his Charbel's sanctuary. Getting there was without conflict.

When we entered the monastery, out of the crowd a monk reached over and shook my hand. It was a long connection, as if we had known each other, and as I walked away, I thought, *This is what it meant to connect with Divine Light.* As if some revelation came through me. I was on holy ground and I was deeply affected.

Saint Charbel was born in 1828 in Lebanon where he had a true Christian upbringing with a passion for prayer. In 1859, he was ordained a priest, and for sixteen years lived his life as a hermit, spending his time praying and worshipping at the Saint Marion's Monastery like his uncles who came before him. While in sermon in December 1898, Charbel was struck by an illness. He suddenly died on Christmas Eve and was buried in the monastery grounds. A few months later dazzling lights appeared around his grave. The monks dug up his corpse and were amazed that his body was still secreting blood and sweat. He was transferred to a special wooden coffin. Hordes of pilgrims began swarming the place to get his intercession, and through this, miracles were experienced while healing incidents amazingly multiplied. This unique phenomenon caused a moral revolution, a return to faith and the reviving of the virtues of the soul.

I walked through the monastery where hundreds and hundreds of Christians from all over the world were swarming the place hoping for a miracle to take over their lives, to connect beyond the norm and feel Charbel's presence within them. I was told by a monk that "These places hold in their memory that which has come before, and man's need to comprehend himself is to tap into that energy that still exists within these walls."

Elevated after having embraced this experience, man feels a step closer to God. I bought some candles and oils to take home to my friends so that in some way by receiving them, something unexpected happens for them through a connection, a belief, a feeling, and a blessing, even in Hollywood. It certainly was for me.

St. Charbel's Monastery. (Author's Collection)

The monastery was a museum in honor of the saint. Displayed behind simple glass partitions that reflected his life were his embroidered clothes, his instruments and vestments of worship, and the visible stains created by his body's secretions still prominently inside his coffin, preserved for all the pilgrims to behold. In a separate room were his books and an altar for prayer, all glowing by the continuously lit candles, preserving the memory and inspiration of a saint who made a difference, a sharp contrast to the atmosphere of tanks and armored cars driving up and down the slopes. In this one little spot, high up in the mountains, peace and loving energy were flourishing. While Michael was making his own discoveries I sat in the garden reflecting on all that had transpired.

Did something change for me in having been here? I think so. After entering unknown and dangerous territories, it was faith once again that opened my heart and mind as it always did on journeys when grace surrounds you. Fear had evaporated. I finally understood what my emotions were about, having witnessed the contrast of war and peace, and the monk whose reaching hand confirmed visible evidence of some invisible event.

My acting teacher Milton Katselas once said that he loved me and I just looked back in silence. "Don't you believe me?" he questioned. "It's in the way you love," I replied. "There is a difference."

Just as here in Lebanon they chose to love each other with a love that's embraced in chaos. It's a struggle inflicted by this war. Most of the people I liked very much, educated, attractive and respectful. I would love to go back as there is much to see in this small piece of earth with its amazing rich heritage.

Now with old fears behind me, and new ones approaching as they always did in times of discovery, I had no intention of getting off this train that carried my love for life's mysteries, knowing that they will always continue to unravel on their own terms.

The Citadel

The Citadel. (Author's Collection)

When powerful men do the unexpected, pivotal moments in history are created. One of those moments is the story that took place in the Middle East during the Third Crusade. Saladin had taken Jerusalem, the most troubled city in history, during the Second Crusade and cleansed the city with rose water. He replaced the cross with the crescent symbolizing Islam and dragged the symbol of the Christian world upside down through the streets of Jerusalem. But now the crusader army under Richard the Lionhearted was confronting the Arab leader in the late 12th century AD. But in that final night, both believing that God was on their side, Richard didn't attack and Saladin chose to hold the city. Why both men did the unexpected remains a great mystery.

As I was studying up on this world, I decided to go back to Egypt and explore the Citadel in Cairo. It was built and completed in 1183 AD. But Saladin never lived in the fortress and left it a year after it was completed. Its location was chosen after a test was made to find the cleanest air in the city. By putting strips of meat in selected spots they could tell how long it took to deteriorate. The raw meat remained the freshest on a hill. Because the quality of air was important, the greatest consideration was the military advantage of the site. Built along the Nile it posed a major threat to any foreign army invading Egypt. It was built with the help of ready-cut stone brought down from the Pyramids of Giza.

I arrived at the Cairo airport and was quickly lined up in front of an X-ray machine to test my health condition. The H1N1 virus was spreading throughout the world and it was a necessary procedure. It seemed to me people would be healthier if they could do something about the horrific smog. I was cleared quickly and met by my guide. When traveling the Middle East I always advise people to work with professionals to eliminate games and uncertainty.

We arrived at the Hyatt Hotel along the Nile. I was given a beautiful room with a great view on the forty-fourth floor where I could see the Citadel at the top of the hill. On a bad day, which is almost every day, the city disappears into the smog and Cairo looks even darker with its mud-like architecture. It's not a pretty sight. But beneath its layers lies an amazing and mysterious history. That's why I love it.

The following day I explored Saladin's world. The fortress was immense, and sounds of the muezzin, distorted and encompassing, filled the air.

I arrived at Muhammad Ali Mosque, built in the early 19th century within the walled city. As usual the shoes come off and you enter a sacred space where people sit on carpets and after prayer discuss their views on life. The domes are magnificent, made of green glass and tile, projecting a beautiful heaven that crowns its faith. When I was once studying to play a terrorist back in Los Angeles, I decided to visit a mosque. I washed my hands and arms in the men's bathroom where others did the same, to be cleansed when they prayed to their God. After the ritual, I came out and stood near where the men began to kneel and pray. To my left women prayed separately. I studied them for about thirty seconds, until a huge guard grabbed me and pinned me against the wall.

"Who are you and why are you looking at our women?" he asked harshly.

I stared him right in the eyes and said, "Is this not a place of God?"

He nodded, "Then behave yourself." It sounded like a line from a movie.

Then calmly I said, "I want to see your superior."

He let go of me and I followed him. I was taken to the back of the mosque where a man, so simple in his demeanor, was reading his Koran. He looked up and asked what he could do for me. Then gestured for me to sit.

"I'm going to play a terrorist and I didn't want to make a cartoon out of him, and so I came here as part of my research," I explained.

He told me some stories, and as I watched him I realized this was very the man I was to play. Simple, without ego, a man connected to his God. I thanked him, smiled at the guard and felt revived. So every time I enter a mosque, I do so respecting their rituals.

Next I found myself with a guide walking the castle streets until I came to the ancient prison. A policeman stepped forward and my guide translated that this area was out of bounds to tourists. I gave him some money and the doors opened up. It never bothered me, as the average Egyptian makes very little money. With his soul satisfied, he let us go through. We came across an old prison that had been smashed to pieces. The tale behind this was that Sadat, the leader of Egypt before Mubarak, was imprisoned here. When he became a modern Pharaoh, Sadat gave freedom to all the prisoners and had the prison condemned. Each cell had been fitted with an iron ball, attached by a chain that held the victims. An ugly sight but obviously the treatment of the prisoners by the authorities was brutal, and because it was inhumane President Sadat had those memories smashed.

The colors that dominated the city were a dirty earth-brown, but some of the moldings and motifs around the ceilings and entrances are painted in the most remarkable colors, cobalt blue, ivory and blood red. Something powerful is encompassed in these walls that holds people's faith together. I stepped out into Saladin Square and sat on the ancient tiles, taking it all in. Perhaps their faith is strong because it's performed five times a day, constantly connecting them to their inner core. And this is manifested physically through its magnificent and glorified monuments. The mystery that remains behind is always there, so when connecting to its hidden source it brings back knowledge of the self. And as one crusader said, "If you can reach that, then you will know wisdom."

In its one thousand years of existence the Citadel had gone through many physical changes, each empire expressing itself differently through its architecture. I visited the palaces built in 1218 AD in the southern enclosure. The rooms were large and very much in the European-inspired style. A little rococo where a gold motif gave it an aura of wealth reflecting a society rich in its façade. Many paintings and portraits adorned the palatial halls and walls. Jewelry was prominent, their facial expressions austere, having been influenced greatly by the Ottoman baroque.

Saladin's strength came from his connection to God, whom he always believed was on his side. In 1185 AD, he was gravely ill, and while on his deathbed, had a revelation to take Jerusalem. He believed God spared him from death to conquer the Holy Land. He called for a Jihad, and a new holy war was born in Jerusalem. This was the city where Mohammad spiritually rose from the rock, and by reminding them of this, Saladin united the Arab world.

After taking Jerusalem he overpowered his enemy and shattered their icons. The remains of the Cross of Jesus had led the Christians into battle, giving them twenty victories. Now that symbol was conquered and Saladin took it to Syria where it disappeared forever.

In the Third Crusade, Richard and his army crossed the European continent for three years to get back from Saladin Christianity's two most prized possessions, the Cross and Jerusalem.

After exploring this moment in history, I concluded that on the eve of his victory Richard knew his men were exhausted and that his army could not sustain holding on to the Holy Land indefinitely. What was also gnawing at him was that his brother John wanted to capture the English crown for himself. Richard turned away from his dream and spared Jerusalem the atrocities that would have transpired.

Saladin, knowing that Richard had the upper hand, was willing to be a martyr. But the unexpected took place, and Saladin believed that God was on his side once again. But slowly Saladin — who was born in Tikrit, Iraq, ironically the same birthplace as Saddam Hussein — was losing his grip and died at the age of fifty-six, six months after Richard had left. Richard never saw Jerusalem and died in battle fighting the French at the age of forty-two. Richard's body had become bloated and exploded into pieces. They say his remains were buried in three different graves. The Christian world never fully recovered.

Finishing my journey, I exited the massive gates and turned back once more to a world where great warriors laid down their lives for their God and the Citadel which encompassed their beliefs and dreams. It was a collision of two faiths and a clash of those symbols — the Crescent and the Cross. Saladin's body was taken back to Damascus where his remains were interred in the great Umayyad Mosque. My curiosity would like to have opened his sarcophagus and witnessed what this great icon's remains looked like and the armor that embraced him in his final hour as a warrior.

On my way to the airport I stopped at the spot where Sadat was assassinated. What a great man Egypt had lost. When I read his spiritual book *In Search of Identity* I was deeply moved by his insights into metaphysics. He was a peaceful warrior. I never felt he was fully appreciated by the Arab world, mainly because he favored the West and brought peace with Israel.

On the other side of the road where his assassination took place a modern pyramid stands with a hollowed center. How ironic that a man who had such compassion and insight for peace in the Middle East should be symbolized by a pyramid with an empty heart.

I left Egypt awakened, certainly grateful and stirred by all that evolved and all the knowledge I had gained. I realized how important it is to know when a journey ends and another begins.

I witnessed on this voyage the beginning of the end for the Mubarak regime. The rumblings had started and another piece of history will have folded. By tapping into that culture's spirit and being there to witness Egypt's new transformation, I gained a better understanding who the Arab Egyptian was becoming while fighting for freedom, and a clearer perception of myself for having walked through it. After all, isn't navigating history's path the reason why we're here?

The Way Out Is The Way Through

On the 28th of June 2008, I arrived at Cairo International Airport to meet with Dr. Zahi Hawass, archaeologist and the Supreme Head of Antiquities of Egypt. Having read many of his books and followed his career through the Los Angeles County Museum of Art, as well as his many guest appearances on Discovery and the History Channel, I felt I had a good grasp of this man. He made a huge difference in bringing to light many of the discoveries of Ancient Egypt onto the world stage.

I arrived in his office punctually at 2 p.m. It was filled with female assistants and surprisingly absent of any Egyptian art.

Walking in, I politely asked, "Are you ready, Dr. Hawass?"

Abruptly he answered, "Ready for what?"

Hmmm, where had all the charm gone? He refused to look up and appeared to be horribly busy. I decided to keep my one-pointedness, as the Zen teachings taught me not to flinch. I began throwing questions at him about Bahariya (Tombs of the Golden Mummies), Seti I (Pharaoh) grandfather of Ramses II, and anything new found in Egypt's largest tomb created for Ramses' sons.

All his answers were an abrupt "No" or equally dismissive. I couldn't seem to reach him. I decided to try another tactic. I remember reading about his friendship with Omar Sharif, whom I had worked with in Europe ten years prior. So I inquired about our mutual friend.

He curtly responded, "He lives in Paris. What else?"

I quickly showed him photos and stories of documentaries I was developing for the Discovery Channel. Immediately I recited a dissertation on the fees that would allow us to shoot in these places. I felt the need to finish this game he was playing, and like an actor knowing his cues, I stood up and quickly finished the meeting with a handshake. At last, a shift took place, and he stood up. I think he was surprised that I had ended the meeting before he had. I was not about to experience his dismissal.

As he gave me his card he said, "You know that only thirty percent of Egyptian artifacts have been uncovered. We have a lot of work ahead of us."

Great, I thought, as I looked into his eyes. I knew I had broken through and my mission was accomplished — the right to explore my journeys in Egypt and have his full approval. I congratulated him for the great work he was doing in Egypt. I thought he may not be the most likable person with his arrogant manner, but I respected him immensely for the great passion and love he has demonstrated toward his country, and making sure nothing — not even a grain of sand — left Egypt without his approval.

Too many European cultures of the 19th century (especially England, France and Germany) looted thousands of artifacts from Egypt and claimed them as their own.

My next journey was to drive to St. Catherine's Monastery at the foot of Mt. Sinai, a seven-hour trek through a desolate environment. This ancient church, fortified by enormous walls protecting over 2,000 icons and over 3,000 manuscripts, is second only to the Vatican library.

Since ancient times the entire area of Sinai has been inhabited by Bedouins (nomads), and it was here that Moses experienced the manifestation of the Divine, where God said, "I am that I am," and charged Moses to free the Israelites from Egypt's bond.

Getting there was difficult. So many security stops. I had mistakenly not taken my passport with me, which was revealed when I entered Egypt legally. My driver had to convince them that I was a tourist having come to meet Dr. Hawass, and so we were allowed to continue on. I wondered why there were so many military and secret police. It was 125 degrees in this hostile environment. The answer would come to me after I had left the country. Through landscapes so desolate and uninviting, I wondered how had Moses survived crossing this desert alone after being thrown into the wilderness by Pharaoh? After eight military stops with the same procedure, being stared at in the backseat by suspicious authority, I just played the role of an innocent in the wild while they tried to stare me down. I survived.

Finally, we arrived before noon. There, a huge number of military police stood firm a hundred yards beneath St. Catherine's Monastery. It was an interrogation scene out of the film *Midnight Express*. The white uniform with the black epaulets, the dark sunglasses and a stance only found in fascist countries where no democracy exists, only fear imposed on the masses. This time my driver's license ID did not suffice.

The head of the police strutted and said to my driver in Arabic, "He will have to go back to Cairo to get his passport. He is not invited here."

My driver translated.

I said to my driver, "This is a Greek monastery ruled over by the Orthodox Church. He is a Muslim and cannot deny me my rights to connect to my God."

He responded in English, "You are persona non grata. Leave."

My driver came up with a brilliant idea to go to the nearest hotel and have the face of my passport faxed from Cairo.

"You wait here," he said.

Along the path to St. Catherine. (Photo: Jack Betts)

I found a shady spot in all that heat, and while waiting for my driver to return I decided to try a different tactic and began charming the police. I found one that spoke Greek, exchanging stories about dreams and women. My driver returned with evidence of my heritage and I was allowed through. Hallelujah!

I trekked the rest of the way on a camel. Uncomfortable as they are, there is something in their motion that connects you to the ancient past where things took time, unlike our modern age. I came across the great wall where Emperor Constantine issued the famous edict that brought an end to the persecution of Christians in 313 AD. He built this monastery around the legendary "burning bush." And it is that tree that still lives after 3,000 years, that continues to give life and purpose to this sanctuary. In all its years of existence, it has never been abandoned.

Arriving at the gates of St. Catherine, I met with Father Porfidios, a journalist who landed here at the age of fifty. He found a place of solitude, became a monk and never looked back. He took me to the well where Moses had met his wife. Sitting at the spot I was spiritually moved and imagined how Moses, having come out of the hostile desert, overcame the death sentence of the Pharaoh. He settled there and became the great myth that still affects the Christian and Muslim faiths. As I walked further into the monastery, I came across the burning bush. Thick in its intensity, I instantly jumped up to grab a piece only to find it covered with fine thorns that seemed to be telling me, "Hands off!" I could imagine after all these hundreds of years this living sacred tree had been cut and gnawed at by the millions of pilgrims over the centuries, feeling it would bring them closer to God — including myself. I left with bleeding fingers. Ouch!

As we sat outside the café, the father began to tell me how the Monastery had been named. In 292 AD an eighteen-year-old woman of royal lineage by the name of Catherine challenged Emperor Maxentius, a worshiper of the pagan gods. By questioning his pagan beliefs, she was sentenced to death. She was put on a water wheel to slowly drown, and to their astonishment the whole thing collapsed. She was finally put to death by decapitation. It is believed that milk — not blood — flowed from her body, and so she was martyred and became the patron saint. In the 19th century, angels guided the monks to her remains in Sinai and buried her within the walls of the great church.

The singular sound of a monk began to echo through the monastery, announcing that four o'clock Mass had begun. I entered the ancient church and the first thing that struck me was the smell of the thousands of candles that had been lit through the ages. I picked one up for myself and put a flame to it. I felt the ancient icons that surrounded me had entered my very being. My seemingly difficult journey in arriving here all of a sudden disappeared, and I could still hear the haunting sounds of their religious mantra echoing in my mind.

The next day, on the way to Damascus, I opened the *Herald Tribune*, and there it was on the front page: an explanation of why I faced so many obstacles getting into Sinai.

The Egyptian security forces had arrested more than a hundred people throughout the country, suspected of plotting terror attacks on the country's treasures. They wrote that three cells, led by operatives outside of Egypt, had allegedly planned bombings in three large cities, espousing an ideology of Takfir, accusing others of apostasy. Large quantities of explosives and weapons were found, as well as maps of official institutions in the country. Egypt's aim was to stop the smuggling of weapons and terrorists through tunnels from Sinai to the Gaza Strip. It cannot afford another threat of terrorism on its soil. Now I understood why my passport was necessary.

In July of 2011, Hawass was fired. Because of Mubarak's downfall and Hawass being part of the old regime, the paper Pharaoh was chased from his office and into his car by hundreds of archaeologists. They screamed at the dictator, calling him an egoist, thief and pretender for standing over their discoveries and making them his own. Having met him, I knew one day that his attitude toward others less fortunate would sting him in the end. He has since disappeared. They say he will be brought to trial. But at the beginning of 2012, I read that Hawass was sentenced to one year in prison on charges of corruption. He is now appealing the verdict. Will he win out or has the Arab winter caught up with him? Only time will tell.

The Burning Bush at St. Catherine's Monastery. (Photo: Jack Betts)

Alexandria
(In Search of Alexander and Cavafy)

As I entered my car the words of Cavafy the poet were singing in my mind again. "Do not hurry the journey at all, it is better to let it last for many years, and to anchor at the island when you are old, rich with all you had become."

It was a Sunday morning and I was on my way to visit the ancient port of Alexandria, where so much history had passed through. The great battles of Julius Caesar in the 1st century BC. Alexander the Great conquering through after crossing the Sahara desert to Siwa, an oasis where he paid homage to the Oracle of Amun and proclaimed himself the son of God. There is a myth that 50,000 Persians tried to cross the same desert after him, but perished. After all, Alexander saw himself as a conquering God. After his battles in Babylon, where he died, his general Ptolemy I brought his remains back to his sacred city and finally buried them there, placed in a great tomb at the crossroads of the city. The tomb's existence remained for five hundred years into the 3rd century AD, where Emperor Caracalla visited his tomb to pay his respects as did Nero, except he stole Alexander's breastplate. Rumor has it that his tomb had been destroyed in the late part of that century. So by the end of the 4th century, the whereabouts of Alexander's tomb had been lost to myth.

In the 19th century, archaeologist Heinrich Schliemann, having already discovered Troy, set his sights on uncovering Alexander's lost tomb. He believed as others did that he was buried beneath the Nabi Daniel Mosque in Alexandria. The Arabs had conquered Egypt in 621 AD, destroying the great library that changed the face of Alexandria's history. Schliemann was denied access to explore the underground city because the mosque was a religious shrine and prominent members of the ruling family were buried nearby. Not able to buy in, he reluctantly left.

My first stop was to visit Nabi Daniel Mosque. The car pulled up and I was surprised to see the simplicity of its architecture, no minarets and no domes. I took my shoes off as was the custom, and because I was not a Muslim I was approached by the custodian of the temple wanting to know what I was doing in Egypt.

"To explore my history," I said.

"Your history?" he asked quizzically.

I told him that it was the ancient culture before the Arab invasion that interested me, the Greeks, the Nubians, the Romans and good old Cleopatra. I also told him the last few years, that Arab history, especially the Crusades, had piqued my interest.

"And who won?" he asked.

To which I replied, "The Arabs, of course."

"That's why you're here, my friend," he replied.

I explained that in 1867 Heinrich Schliemann believed that Alexander was buried beneath this mosque. As I shook his hand I placed a $20 bill in it. He smiled and gestured for me to follow him. I love traditions.

I entered the mosque and there in the middle of it was a large gaping hole. He explained that a few years ago while a workman was polishing the granite floor it collapsed beneath him. He took me down by ladder, and there I found myself walking on the grounds of 1st-century Alexandria. The smell of the moist earth permeated the damp cool air. We used a flashlight as we made our way into the past. There were a lot of tombs that had been looted, but I thought, Where be Alexander?

The keeper mentioned that the underground complex went deeper into the abyss but was dangerous to enter due to its fragile state. Schliemann would have been disappointed, as I was, but I still felt I was in a sacred place beneath a 19th-century metropolis. As we came back into the light the custodian mentioned that new excavations were taking place in the Christian and Jewish cemeteries on Anubis Street, and they now believe that it is the true burial site of Alexander. I thanked him and instructed my guide that our next stop would be Anubis Street.

We arrived at the cemetery and after going through a maze of tombstones discovered an alabaster tomb with natural decorations covering its entrance. There were lots of workmen digging large trenches as I inconspicuously entered the tomb. I discovered that this structure was merely the antechamber to a large underground tomb. It may have been the Soma where Ptolemy interred Alexander the Great. I spoke to one of the archaeologists who told me that they are now focusing on this impressive underground complex. From our clipped conversation I discerned that this space belonged to someone of great importance and possibly it is the Soma itself, the lost tomb of Alexander. They had dug down ten meters below the surface, and what they are hoping to discover one day could possibly be the greatest find of the century.

At least three miles of Alexandria's coastline has been subjected to earthquakes and tsunamis, and many of its seaports have disappeared beneath the sea. But at the moment a lot of excitement has taken place where forty miles out of Alexandria the tombs of Antony and Cleopatra may have been discovered in an area called Taposiris Magna, but that excavation is out of bounds. As for Alexander, the excavations continue. And yet some cynics suggest that in the end Alexander the Great found a watery grave beneath the Mediterranean, buried there not by man but by nature's powers. But the romance continues.

That evening I stayed at the Cecil Hotel, an icon of Alexandria, where in the late 19th and early 20th centuries great writers like Durrell, E.M. Forster, Auden and Cavafy spent time exploring this exotic world. Their words were drawn from the whole of the city's past and present and created their own personal vision.

The next morning I was anxious to see Cavafy's house, which had been converted into a museum. He was one of the great poets of the 20th century. It was located at 4 Sharm el-Sheikh. I entered his apartment building, and while I was climbing the stairs I recalled something he said in his biography. Looking out from the balcony of his flat, where he lived for the last twenty-five years of his life, till 1933, he wrote, "Where could I live better? Below, the brothel caters to the flesh, and over there is the church which forgives sins, and over there is a hospital where we die." The bordello is long gone but the old Greek hospital, where he died, is still standing.

Outside Cavafy's residence. (Author's Collection)

I knocked on the door of his flat and Mohammad, the keeper of the museum, welcomed me. The sound of a 1940s opera singer spoke his poem "Ithaca" in Greek, melodiously filling the entire house. I remembered that even Jacqueline Kennedy requested that it be read at the end of her journey. It seems the older I get the better I understand it. After all, it is about the voyage of life.

Ithaca

When you set out on your journey to Ithaca,
Pray that the road is long,
full of adventure, full of knowledge.
The Lestrygonians and the Cyclops,
The angry Poseidon ... do not fear them:
You will never find such as these on your path,
If your thoughts remain lofty, if a fine
emotion touches your spirit and your body.
The Lestrygonians and the Cyclops,
The fierce Poseidon you will never encounter,
If you do not carry them within your soul,
If your soul does not set them up before you.

Pray that the road is long.
That the summer mornings are many, when,
with such pleasure, with such joy
you will enter ports seen for the first time;
Stop at Phoenician markets,
And purchase fine merchandise,
Mother-of-pearl and coral, amber and ebony,
and sensual perfumes of all kinds,
as many sensual perfumes as you can;
Visit many Egyptian cities,
to learn and learn from scholars.

Always keep Ithaca in your mind.
To arrive there is your ultimate goal.
But do not hurry the voyage at all.
It is better to let it last for many years;
And to anchor at the island when you are old,
Rich with all you have gained on the way,
Not expecting that Ithaca will offer you riches.

Ithaca has given you the beautiful voyage.
Without her you would have never set out on the road.
She has nothing more to give you.

And if you find her poor, Ithaca has not deceived you.
Wise as you have become, with so much experience,
You must already have understood what Ithacas mean.

—Constantine P. Cavafy (1911)

Reading at Cavafy's Desk. (Author's Collection)

As I walked into Cavafy's office and sat at his Victorian desk where he wrote his poetry, I gazed out the window and took in the surroundings. The sheer curtains suddenly flew open.

"Ah, was that his spirit entering the room, after having been at a local bar observing his beautiful people, young and old?" I chuckled.

Then sadness when I felt he had gone.

I walked through the rest of the house and into his bedroom, with its brass bed and the intricate lace that covered it just as he had left it — so Greek, so simple and traditional. I lay down on his bed and took in the ambience. I felt blessed and yet a sudden loneliness came over me. Is this what he felt in his final days and why his poems had a tinge of melancholy? My thoughts were interrupted by the caretaker who asked me to sign the guest book. As I did, I noticed that above my signature was the name of the president of Greece, Karamanlis. Then a group of young students entered and I thought he would have been pleased by the influence he had had on such a varied group of people.

Just before I left the room, I turned and whispered, "Thank you, I now realize what Ithacas meant."

It's about anyone on a life's journey. He says not to obsess too much on the obstacles before you, to keep you from the riches that await you. If you don't own them they cannot defeat you. The poet advises to enjoy all that comes your way. The final insight is the acceptance of the life you have lived. I read that when Cavafy died he drew a circle on a piece of paper and then placed a period in its center. Was that God's eye? He seemed complete.

I read an article by G.W. Bowerstock who said that in the summer of 1932 when Cavafy's death drew near, his friends persuaded him to go to Athens for treatment of throat cancer, only recently diagnosed. He attracted many notables who wasted no time in revealing what they learned, even though after a tracheotomy Cavafy was no longer able to speak at all. His last observations had to be transmitted by way of penciled notes. He returned back to Alexandria in 1932 and died the following April.

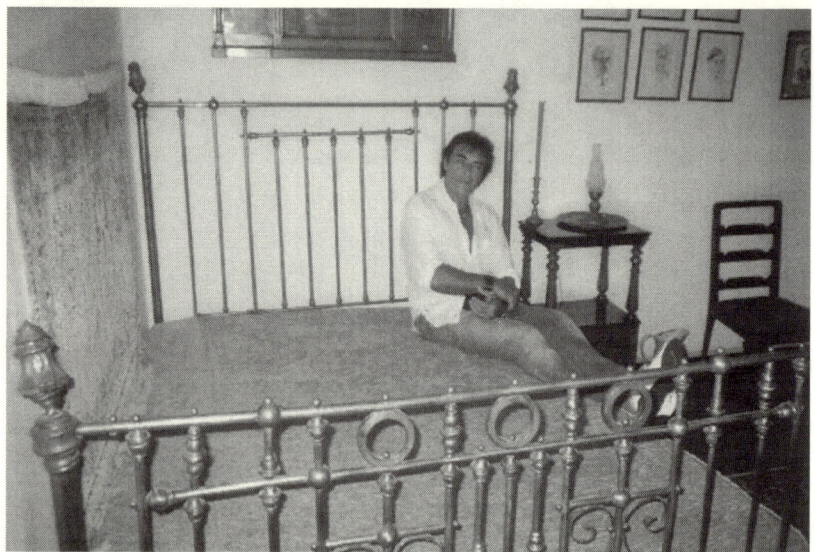

Cavafy's bedroom. (Author's Collection)

The God Abandons Antony

When at the hour of midnight
An invisible choir is suddenly heard passing
With exquisite music, with voices —
Do not lament your fortune that at last subsides,
Your life's work that has failed, your schemes that have proved illusions.
Back like a man prepared, like a brave man,
Bid farewell to her, to Alexandria who is departing.
Above all, do not delude yourself; do not say that it is a dream,
That your ear was mistaken.
Do not condescend to such empty hopes.
Like a man for long prepared, like a brave man,
Like to the man who was worthy of such a city,
Go to the window firmly,
And listen with emotion,
But not with the prayers and complaint of a coward
Listen to the notes, to the exquisite instruments of the mystic choir,
And bid farewell to her, to Alexandria whom you are losing.

—Cavafy

In the Greek Orthodox cemetery in Alexandria, written on his tombstone is a simple inscription: "Poet."

It was all so personal. I felt that I had visited a past relative whose ghost was still haunted by his own words. So I decided to end my day reflecting along the concourse that paralleled the Mediterranean. While facing the ocean's turmoil there was a lot to think about, remembering how much of its history had been swallowed up and the mysteries that still remained beneath it. The answers will surface eventually, but for now Egypt is more in search of a modern resolution than its established past.

Into Enemy Territory

Every time I brought up the idea of going to Syria my friends (and even my agent) thought I was insane. I had become an American citizen in 2008 and wanted to know what it was like to travel as an American abroad.

As an arch foe of Israel and the United States, this fascinating region of the Middle East had some of the most bloodied history pass through its landscape. In 2008, Damascus was named the Arab Capital of Culture. Egyptians, Greeks, Romans, Ottomans and the crusaders all carved out their signatures in this cradle of civilization, leaving behind an amazing array of excavated sites and artifacts. It's unbelievable to think that 70 percent of Syria's history still remains buried in the sand. My plan was to go and explore Damascus, then on to the great castle Krak Des Chevaliers, and finally to the ancient ruins at Palmyra.

In the summer of 2009, ignoring everyone's advice, I arrived at Damascus International Airport. I stood in line for almost two hours before I reached the immigration officials. Even then they kept everyone waiting while they conversed in Arabic, not giving a damn about the people suffering in this stifling heat and having traveled for thousands of miles. I was finally called and I handed over my American passport, and that's when the three officials looked up and studied me with apparent disdain. They asked me the usual questions concerning what interests brought me to their country.

My response was:

"The wonderful history of Islam, and being of Greek heritage I wanted to visit the ancient city of Palmyra."

"Wasn't Palmyra Roman?" they asked.

"Yes, but it was Greek first, in the 2nd century BC and a very important Christian site during the Roman and Nabataean occupation," I replied.

They just stared. It's moments like this that ratified my decision to always travel with the knowledge of the culture I am visiting, and making sure nothing in my bags would raise unnecessary attention in case I got searched. And that for me is constant. I tried to make more conversation about being in their country for the first time, but they were not interested. And with that, their final stroke was stamping my passport, and throwing it back in my face. Not wanting a provocation, I simply said, "Thank you," picked up my bag and exited. Finally I was in.

Standing in the light, again. Krak des Chevaliers Castle. (Author's Collection)

It wasn't difficult finding a cab, as they all came swarming toward me, shouting their "special" offers. I made a choice and off to my hotel I went, thirty minutes away to the center of Damascus.

At the front desk the female clerk ushered me through the usual arrival routine. I signed in and handed over my American Express card, which she refused.

"In Syria we don't take this card."

"What about traveler's checks?" I asked.

"No, no, no," she said, "American Express is persona non grata in my country." Why didn't I know this?

"Get me American Express on the phone, please," I said.

She just stared.

"Isn't that the reason why you sit on that side of the counter?"

Love was not flowing. Reluctantly she picked up the phone and dialed, handing it over to me when they answered. They were apologetic, explaining that the circumstances between U.S./Syrian relationships faltered, so they were no longer doing business there. I liked this company because if anything goes wrong with purchases, American Express always backs you. So I had no choice but to use another card. The concierge smirked when I handed it to her.

My room was not quite ready, so I decided to walk around the streets by my hotel. I took in the atmosphere of this lovely city surrounded by mountains, its multicultural façades from different periods of its history, the sounds of the mosques and the always dependable jewelry stores, the people strolling by arm in arm, even the men; I began to get excited being in Damascus, one of the oldest continuously inhabited cities in the world. The only drawback was its ruthless government led by the Assad family, who had been in power since 1971 and still dominated this region. Syrians have endured decades of economic hardship, political repression and corruption under this family's rule, yet it still continues today to jail critics of its regime, also having a stranglehold on the Internet and the media. There are rats in the walls and they have ears, and if you are ever arrested, God help you in those filthy prisons and what these people are capable of doing to you. It was not a movie where the hero walks away in the end, so I decided to trust no one. I was to tread lightly, never taking anything for granted.

I went back to my hotel and found my room ready. When I entered the elevator another man followed me in. I pressed the eighth-floor button and he didn't move, except through the elevator mirror I caught him scrutinizing me. I thought, Oh, yes, secret police, here we go again. He either sensed I was foreign by my dress, or someone in the hotel informed him I was American. Not too many of us venture into this part of the world, so when we do, a red flag goes up. Getting out of the elevator I insisted he go first. Reluctantly he did and acted out as if he was looking for something until I entered my room. I waved a sad goodbye and he uncomfortably did the same. I had a good laugh, letting him know I was on to him.

Later that evening when I was entering the elevator, to my surprise the same secret policeman was waiting. As the doors shut I asked him if he was following me.

"I don't speak your language," he said.

"Pity, we could have had such fun," I said as the doors opened.

He nodded and left. They always seem to suspect foreigners when they travel alone. I've had encounters before with secret police, especially in Egypt where they always believe you're guilty of something or just simply suspicious. Nothing to hide, I went into one of the hotel's restaurants to meet my guide, Amir, with whom I had connected through the Internet. He turned out to be a prize.

We sat in the restaurant for two hours discussing the best way to approach my interests. He was a Christian who struggled with the present government. He referred to Syria's leader as the "Sphinx" as many of his people thought of him as an enigma, with a reputation as a wily and able politician but a man who could also be manipulative and merciless, especially with those who opposed his regime. He was involved in terrorist training, with a pool of individuals willing to carry out certain violent missions. Stretching its arms, Syria was key to the Palestinian problem and at the vortex of the Lebanese situation. It acted as a bridge for arms smuggling from Iran into Lebanon for Hezbollah, influencing the outcome of the Israeli/Lebanese war and the assassination of the Lebanese Prime Minister Rafik Hariri in 2005. It seems the Middle East has been at war its entire history, with Iran always stirring the pot. And here I was sitting in the atmosphere of this political drama, with danger always lurking in the shadows.

The next day we decided to venture out to the Umayyad Mosque. This magnificent structure, built in 705 AD with golden mosaics and three tall minarets, houses the final resting place of the most famous Arab leader, Saladin, who originally came from Tikrit in Iraq and was responsible for uniting the Arab world. Next to Mohammed, he is the most revered man in Syria. A military leader who conquered Jerusalem in the Second Crusade of the 12th century AD and brought new light and power to the Muslim world. A simple red-domed mausoleum built in 1193 contains his remains.

When I arrived that morning I was amazed to see the mosque so crowded. After I took off my shoes and entered the courtyard I could not believe its beauty. So pristine, its luminous marbled facing shone in the light like a jewel, with entire families sitting around the square conversing in peace. Its splendor ranks with Jerusalem's Dome of the Rock, while in sanctity is second only to the holy mosques of Mecca and Medina. As I walked into the mosque hundreds of men were kneeling down praying directly to Allah. I loved the ceremony, everyone praying in unison to the sounds of the muezzins, and not a conflict in sight. In the middle of the mosque was a huge ornamented basilica. To my surprise Amir told me that part of the head of John the Baptist was laying within the tomb, contained in a casket here. I peered through the veiled windows, but the outline of the remains was blurred due to the dim light, and as in many of the Tales of Islam, the mystery remains. But I sat around the mosque with its people and studied their behavior, their women veiled, my eyes remembering never to stare long enough to draw attention.

After lunch our next stop was the Old City Quarter, where miles of winding labyrinthine-like alleys epitomize the city's charm. It's exhausting finding your way through, but we finally came upon the Christian Quarter where the church of St. Ananias stands, built over the site of St. Paul's escape from an attempted murder. Before he converted as an Apostle of Christ, Paul was a Roman soldier who persecuted Christians, found faith and became a staunch advocate of Christianity. If Paul of Tarsus had not spoken Greek or understood the Greek expression of love and if he had not spread that word, then Christianity might have remained a minor Jewish heresy. He was eventually beheaded in Rome for spreading the gospel.

We walked down the ancient steps to the underground chapel of St. Ananias, who had baptized Paul at the spot where an altar stands. St. Ananias became head of the local Christians and a prominent leader of the Apostolic Age. While on missionary work in Syria, Ananias was arrested at the order of Governor Licinius for preaching Christianity and stoned to death outside the walls of Damascus. I sat down on a bench and thought about how many Christians had suffered under Roman authority; even the Apostles of Christ met with a ghastly end. I never understood why religion caused so much chaos. After all, we are supposed to believe in the same God, but the ways of connecting to him cause so much friction.

I remember someone from the Jewish faith asked me once, "Why do you Christians have to pray to icons to reach God? We just simply pray to HIM."

I remarked, "I didn't know God had a direct line." There was no argument.

I felt the ancient stone walls of the simple church, and after 2,000 years the memories that remain within them must be frightening, but then also euphoric. So I remained for an hour quietly meditating, lit some candles and left feeling quite sad.

With so much brutality and suffering in the world, where was God? It sometimes made me question my religion, because the answers are usually blank no matter how many times your local priest tried to explain his version of the gospel. In the end you still walk alone and occasionally a beam of light strikes you and re-establishes faith.

Amir gave me a tour of the city, its museums and landmarks, and what impressed me the most was the Souk, where Middle Eastern wares are sold. Damascus was an important caravan city with the trade routes from southern Arabia, Palmyra, Petra, and the Silk Road from China all converging on it. The city has been built up with every passing occupation and it has been difficult to excavate the ruins that lie at least ten feet below the modern level, just like Alexandria, Rome and Athens.

We came to the entrance of the Souk, a massive marketplace covered with a corrugated roof, selling everything from clothing, jewelry and carpets, and their famous ice-cream parlors and the always curious salesman trying to lure tourists and the locals into his shop. One thing that stood out was the dappled lighting effect by the sun streaming in through hundreds of bullet holes in the roof. It was caused by celebrating Arab riflemen after the Ottomans and the Germans retreated in 1917 and by machine guns from French planes firing down on Syrian rebels in 1925. I loved the atmosphere that it offered, like stars from heaven pouring down on you.

The people were very friendly and continued to be as I got more into my journey, certainly a contrast to my beginnings. I explored the amazing colors of the spices stacked up like jewels, and smelled their pungent odor. The chef in me was fired up, but I didn't buy anything to bring home as customs in the U.S. are strict about foreign food products. I ended up buying some of their ice cream, rich in cream and rolled in pistachio nuts. It was delicious. I was tempted to buy some beautifully made jewelry in lapis and some silverware, but a voice kept telling me you don't need anything. Carrying merchandise can be exhausting when traveling, as we all know, but when you come back home, they become part of the memories that you reveal in the conversations you shared with friends over dinner.

Coming out into the sunshine, on the other side of the Souk stood the columns and arches that were the remains of the Temple of Jupiter, reminding me of the powerful Roman era with the eastern foothills as its backdrop. What a setting, taking in the modern and ancient architecture. I just loved how well the contrast worked. So intriguing, so mysterious and rich are these bloody worlds of past eras. And there, a short distance away, was a huge poster of Assad the Sphinx dominating the landscape. The image reminded me how little would shift as long as that dictator was in power. But nothing really has changed since ancient times, when previous leaders built replicas of themselves too, to remind its people daily who was their god, never believing one day their statues and images would crumble and disappear into the sand. It was a full day and it was time to go back to the hotel.

Our next journey was the legendary Krak des Chevaliers in Hama, three hours outside of Damascus. We began early, driving through hilly regions and deserts until we discovered the castle in the distance reaching a summit of 750 meters above sea level. The height and size were spectacular. The fortress was completed in the early 12th century, built to control a strategic passage called the Homs Gap in the Orontes Valley. It was to highlight Christian power, a symbol that the conquerors were here to stay. The Crusades were a collision of two faiths, the Crescent and the Cross, both believing God was on their side.

We drove up the steep terrain until we reached the top of the hill in front of its enormous gates. From the outside the fortress was powerful and intimidating. As I slowly walked through the castle I couldn't help but feel the memories of their wars coming at me, and the sounds of horses' hooves, back from war, echoed through the chambers. Those energies were left behind in the shadows of dark corridors, for theirs was a brutal life, bloody fighting for their Jihad, serving God and longing for enlightenment. I came across a secret chamber that led down into the gallows of the castle, and supposedly the tunnels end two miles away into a Christian church called St. George. It was a route the Crusaders used to enter and escape from the enemy. But the passageway was closed off now because it was in danger of collapsing.

I moved further into the castle until I arrived at the Hall of the Knights, which included a well, a bakery and the latrines. The chambers that held the kitchens were enormous, where large pots were used to cook and feed the hundreds of soldiers, and always hold a five-year stock of provisions in case of siege. I sat there imagining the raucous conversations reverberating through those fortified walls, how they withstood the numerous Arab assaults during their more than two hundred years of occupation. Because of its impenetrable walls those knights lived securely within the castle. I went down to the moat, full of algae, and above its exit door lying between those thick grey walls was an emblem with the name Richard the Lionhearted, King of England. He was a devout Christian but a brutal leader in his battles against Saladin.

Inside the Souk, Damascus. (Author's Collection)

Krak des Chevaliers Castle, Syria. (Author's Collection)

On top of Krak des Chevaliers. (Author's Collection)

I couldn't wait to reach the top so I could witness how the Crusaders watched their enemies approaching. Running up the stairs, two steps at a time, I kept reminding myself I was still an athlete. Being in this battleground, ancient as it was, still brought out the warrior in me. Reaching the castle's highest point, I stretched out my arms and called out to the universe. Men created steeples built on top of mountains because it brought them closer to God. And on top of this castle, I experienced that feeling. What a view they had, so clear that I could see Lebanon in the distance. My guide directed me down to the moat and the drawbridge that was used to obstruct the enemy. Just like in the movies, where the hero saves and kisses the maiden in the end, but that was Hollywood. Though here there was not a woman in sight. It's as if they did not exist in the Crusaders' world or in the world of Islam. Lust left no trace.

Then we explored the monolithic stone walls, a castle within a castle, and the inner fortress higher than the outside structure so the defenders could always dominate their enemy from a superior height. There were strategic openings in the walls, allowing the knights to shower their enemy with their ammunition of arrows, rocks and flaming pitch.

In 1188, Saladin came to conquer the infidels, examined its defenses, and because of its impenetrable might, decided to move on without attempting to besiege it. Even Lawrence of Arabia tried to scale the walls barefoot in 1909 but only made it halfway to the top. Like all mighty powers through history, the end always shows its recognizable face.

In 1271, with only two hundred knights left, the Christian warriors surrendered their mighty stronghold to the Muslim forces. Within twenty years after Krak des Chevaliers fell, the Crusaders withdrew from the Holy Land completely.

As we were leaving, a summer classical concert was being prepared. Hearing those aesthetics in this environment was such a contrast to the sounds of war from the past. In a castle that brutally shed so many lives, eight hundred years later it became a forum where the beauty of music permeated through its hardened walls, instead of the loud cries of dying men.

On the way back to Damascus, Amir suggested we visit an ancient village called Maaloula ("Entrance") where the language of Christ, Aramaic, was still spoken. When we entered the village its religious heritage was evident in this oasis in the midst of a desert. A large statue of the Virgin Mary dominated the rugged hillside at an altitude of 1,500 meters, a Christian site with 2,000 inhabitants, which refused to be swallowed up by the Muslim world at its doorstep.

When we arrived at a monastery, the church within had a very simple entrance. One of the oldest in the Christian world dating from 296 AD, its foyer with three arches was filled with icons. I lit three candles, one each for my family, this country and for my safe passage through. As I took in the church, which was stunning, I pulled out my camera and was advised that no photos were allowed, something to do with people using duplicates for profit. The beautiful woman who was the keeper of this shrine saw my disappointment and volunteered to recite the Lord's Prayer in Aramaic. Guilt. She guided us up to the simple stone altar, which had no rim or drain spout, a sign that it was never used for bloody sacrifices. She began the prayer, which was so foreign in sound, yet within me I recognized the rhythm. She was such an innocent in contrast to the exploration I experienced at the barracks of Krak des Chevaliers. There, everything was about death, and here in this little sanctum some simple, loving thoughts were being shared. I kept thinking, where is the enemy?

I explored the church, touching everything as I typically do to connect the innocence of icons and its ancient walls while burning candles gave off light. I certainly was in God's territory. We sat for a while and watched an ancient race of people behaving in the same way their ancestors did for 1,500 years. Simple. These are moments in life that stay with you, touching off memories, something familiar, like having lived there before. All I knew was each day brought me closer to myself, and the fear of the unknown seemed to be dropping away.

After leaving the church I decided to walk around the village. The ancient rock formations were so mysterious that every corner I turned became another expression of art. Its colors were vibrant and whole families filled the spaces, enjoying a picnic lunch. One family, curious about my presence, invited me to join them. Happily I took the opportunity to break bread with a society unknown to me. And I was in my element, like it was an audition. They spoke very little English but my animated behavior broke through the barriers. A plate of mezeh was handed to me like I was family and we communicated as best we could. Curious about my American citizenship, but feeling familiar because of my Greek heritage with theirs, we found a common ground. It's the leadership that gives the country its reputation to the rest of the world, and we judge its people for it. But here I was seeing their hearts through my own eyes, and what a joyful and insightful experience it was. When it was time to leave they all stood respectfully to embrace, and I parted knowing that a little more peace was shared.

It was back to Damascus as it was getting late. I had a quiet dinner at the hotel where now everyone was smiling. I must have been touched by grace. I read up on my next and last venture to the amazing ruins of ancient Palmyra (the Place of Palms) three hours outside of the city. It was early and hot the next morning when we saddled up for our last odyssey in Syria. I was in my element, feeling like a Bedouin crossing the desert with water by my side, a rolled cigarette burning and Syrian music stirring the atmosphere.

When we arrived the city shone like a jewel in the distance, golden in color like the sand it stood upon. We got out and started to walk through the ruins. The main axis of the city of Palmyra was the colonnaded road, with its forest of columns and its shining roofs of gilded bronze, running from north to south, and expanded in the 2nd century AD. The city came under Greek influence because of Alexander the Great and his expansionist policies. But its power lay because of its crucial position as a caravan center along the Silk Route, reaching enormous heights during the Roman occupation and its demand for luxury goods.

Palmyra became an aristocratic republic and found its independence in 261 AD, but ten years later the Roman Aurelian put the city to fire and sword. It was eventually conquered again by the Arabs in 638 AD and burnt to the ground. A castle built during the Crusades stood high up on a ridge looking down on the places it conquered. Wars have destroyed so much beauty, but the remains are some of the greatest ruins I have ever walked through. What is still visible of its conquered past are the influences of the great societies that molded it.

A view from the great Crusader Castle. (Author's Collection)

When I saw the beautiful amphitheater I made my entrance, the same way the entertainers of the past did, and imagined the applause, taking a bow after reciting some Shakespeare. To my surprise some real applause echoed through from the tourists above, and we all had a good laugh. I had hoped it wasn't the performance. Nothing like a humble actor finding his audience in a desert landscape. No pay, just an inner reward adding to the many memories I had collected. A man interrupted the impromptu revelry, telling me it was time to hop on a camel. I wasn't ready to leave just yet. "Later," I said.

As I visited the many tombs, I discovered such beauty in the expression of how they perceived life and death through the intricate detail of their art. Many statues draped over marble coffins, still in their original color after 2,000 years, and on its walls, their stories written in ancient verse, all so beautifully preserved by this desert landscape.

I overheard an archaeologist speaking to some tourists, "From the air using infrared technology, they discovered that beneath the sands are hundreds of uncovered tombs. The Japanese team analyzed images from satellites orbiting 700 kilometers above the earth, and the results were extraordinary."

Wow, I thought. So much wealth, so many secrets still waiting to surface to bring further light to this remarkable heritage. And credit must be given to the Japanese archaeologists who investigated and researched a lot of this history. I thought it interesting that archaeologists from a Japanese culture were excavating Middle Eastern life, and they were doing remarkable work.

Now it was time to ride a camel in this hot atmosphere. It was 130 degrees and thank God for my hat. There was no shade at all, just tall columns and some of their fallen remains due to war and earthquakes. I mounted a temperamental camel that kept growling at me. He must have sensed I was foreign. I kept saying to him, "I know we're at war." The growling got louder.

And so I began the last phase of the journey along the colonnaded street. How they must have felt during their golden years, surrounded by such beauty with their mythical heroes coming back from war, parading their victories past the shouting mob. Suddenly the roar of a motorcycle whizzed by and stopped, abruptly spraying all of us with sand. The camel got very upset and began to ride off with me dangling halfway off my saddle. But the owner ran after us and took hold of the camel's rein while he began shouting at the man on the motorcycle.

He abruptly responded to me, "I was the one who asked you to ride my camel first, but you are not a man of your word, you said, 'Later.'" He roared off screaming, "See you in the next life."

"Yes," I shouted back, "hopefully you'll come back as a camel, so I can kick your ass."

So much for hospitality. I let it go and finished my trek through the colonnaded street with ease.

Back to the car, it was time to return to my hotel and pack for tomorrow's flight at 3 a.m. Feeling grateful for having survived my experiences through Syria and navigating my exit out of the country without scrutiny, I boarded my flight to Los Angeles through Russia with an eight-hour layover. Waiting at the Moscow terminal was not without incident because while resting some pickpocket lifted my wallet from my jacket. Eventually I had a laugh over it, as there was no money inside.

I had time to reflect what had transpired in Syria. I was happy with the outcome and the people I met along the way. They were good people, just caught up in a world that was lagging behind the rest of us.

But now as I write this passage in 2013, Syria, like the rest of the Middle East, is going through a huge transformation, its people battling through their city streets demanding that their voices are heard. The Assad government is behaving like thugs, while fighting and murdering its own people to survive this revolution. A human rights report was issued accusing Syrian security forces of committing crimes against humanity.

Syrian security forces have been killing and torturing their own people with complete impunity. Assad will be facing the same consequences as Mubarak is in prison in Egypt facing a trial for crimes against humanity. If convicted, he would be facing the death penalty. I hope that the people's cry in Syria will be heard in a democratic fashion so they can have the freedom and opportunity that is their right to become who they truly are, as we are blessed in the West.

I'm so glad I went to Syria and the Middle East before the revolution, because when I do go back to make new discoveries, and with the old enemy conquered, it will be seen through new eyes.

Sunset at Giza

Arriving in July 2010, the light in Cairo was dimmed by the usual smog. It clouded the area, giving off a strange hue that accentuated the mystery of this veiled city. On both sides of the main thoroughfare leading into the metropolis were secret police every thirty yards. My driver said that the president was arriving from Sharm el-Sheikh. Since President Mubarak witnessed Sadat's murder in October of 1981 and was the only man left standing, he had a great fear of being assassinated. He surrounded himself with the military 24/7. If the gods were talking to him and he was listening, he would have heard that he would be overthrown by year's end. As with all dictators, their pockets deep, their people's lives controlled and their dreams suppressed, the youth of Egypt finally exploded. After forty years of tyranny another modern-day Pharaoh's reign collapsed. And so began the revolution. But this was July and those historical circumstances hadn't yet arrived.

I was eager to see the three great Pyramids of the Giza plateau at sunset on the West Bank of the Nile, the last of the Seven Wonders of the ancient world. I was met by my driver, Hani, who suggested I have a session with Gamal, a healer who works with essential oils — concentrated hydrophobic liquid containing volatile aroma compounds from plants. Then fully relaxed, I would take the journey to the Pyramids at sunset where the local Egyptian cowboys would serve dinner. It sounded like a joke, but they do exist. Well, I thought, that's what journeys are about, being available for the unexpected and being part of an ancient heritage that still perplexes the world by the scale of its creation.

Gamal introduced himself and took me to his place of healing, filled with hundreds of bottles of essential oils. He was a most trustworthy man. His eyes gently stared right back at me, unlike some of the dealers here — first the money, and then you're at their mercy. The trick is never to flinch when deals are being placed as it questions your manhood.

Stripped to my underwear, I lay down on my stomach as Gamal very intensely rubbed lotus oil all over me. The aroma was wonderfully pungent. Then he turned me over on my back and did the same. Without hesitation I slipped into a meditation, landing in my mind's eye that flashed a bearded male on a camel. Then a cloud crossed my face and quickly disappeared. The same image kept repeating itself, and each time the vision came closer and more focused. My God, it was I in another time, with a beard, dressed in robes. Me, Egyptian? Is that why I keep coming back to Egypt and feeling at home? Why certain memories lingered? Why

I kept having a sense of déjà vu? I became so still, so enveloped in my past visions that I didn't want to resurface. I could hear soft lamentations accompanying the ritual, like a chorus floating over me. After it stopped I began to slowly emerge out of this unexpected revelation.

When I awoke I was surprised to find what seemed like ten minutes was over an hour in time. Gamal had a smile on his face, and said, "You went into a past life, around 2800 BC. You were a merchant who was born in Luxor and eventually moved to Cairo. You keep coming back here because you love this country and you have unresolved issues of your past."

"Like what?" I asked.

"They will be revealed when you are ready, and when you are satisfied you will let go and move forward."

It was fascinating, especially when he said "merchant." My great-grandparents and our ancestors before them were merchants in Constantinople. Maybe that's why I like dealing with Arabs in business. My attitude is, "Don't screw with me, I've met bigger crooks in Hollywood." Feeling totally relaxed and vulnerable I was open to my next adventure — getting on a camel and riding into the desert before the light disappeared.

So with my friends Gamal and Hani, I rode behind the Pyramids where all the animals, donkeys, camels and horses are fed and stabled. As I learned from my experience in Syria, camels are not the most pleasant animals to ride. I love the rhythm in the heat, it made me feel like to a warrior in a desert, but it's the hundreds of flies that hover around the camel's head that bugs me. Also they have this temperament that you can't always trust, and when they get on their high horse they love to kick and the occasional spit is thrown your way as well. I have been subjected to all of this and responded by kicking them back. I always did make friends in such high places.

For an hour and a half we rode into an area few travelers get a chance to see. A desert that was once very green during the Golden Age of the Pyramids, but now it is very dry with not a single palm tree in sight. This arid area was created around 2200 BC. A dramatic pattern in the weather brought about drastic measures that changed the face of Egypt. This magnificent country suffered terribly, bringing it to its knees. And thus the desert was created and it wasn't until 1800 BC that Egypt raised itself again and created its new Golden Age.

All of this was going through my mind as we entered a landscape I will never forget. We climbed the sand dunes, and there they were, the last of the Ancient Wonders. Menkaure, Khafre and Khufu, resurrection machines, and in that transformation the Pharaoh became a gloried being of light, effective in the afterlife. Once mummified and the Pharaoh entombed, it set the cosmic engine in motion. It was a meeting point of life and light with death and darkness so they could travel the underworld and eventually join the ranks of the gods. What a process.

It was now 7 p.m. and the intense sun was hovering over the desert when a blasting sound of Middle Eastern music screamed from a stereo. A woman covered in total black with no face exposed except for the eyes was being driven in a horse carriage. I jumped off my camel and yelled at the driver to bring the sound down. The lady in black stared at me, and it was her posture as she stood that revealed her disapproval. This was her country, and it is the way they reveal their discord. I tried to explain the beauty we were experiencing and that silence was necessary to understand what our senses were trying to perceive. That noise pollution was an obliteration of our spirit. She sat down and reluctantly instructed the driver to move on without the noise. "Thank you," I said with a smile.

I returned to my camel and we continued on. There in the distance on my left was a lone figure dressed in a white galabeya and keffiyeh with the wind blowing his costume so freely that it reminded me of Lawrence of Arabia. It was so surreal that it almost felt like an illusion that deserts have been known to create. What a contrast to the noise a few minutes ago. One being connected to the life presented while the other was unconscious to the elements. The Lawrence figure was enjoying the solitude, while the woman in black was trying to make a stand in a male-dominated society.

We had now reached the highest sand hill where the view of the Pyramids was breathtaking. The light from the sunset was a glowing pink, giving the monoliths an aura of mystery. Gamal got off his camel and instructed us to follow him. Reaching the edge of the sand hills, he asked that we simply remain silent and keep an eye on the largest Pyramid of Cheops and just observe the illusion. If we're lucky some figures or ghosts from its distant past will appear. He believed they were the keepers of the monuments. He asked us not to question but to trust that whatever we witnessed was not an apparition. After the past-life regression I had experienced that afternoon I was up for anything. Within fifteen minutes something appeared coming out of the largest pyramid. My eyes saw these black figures as ghostlike in their movements. The vision continued for ten minutes and then disappeared. I looked at Gamal and he smiled knowingly.

He said, "I just wanted you to see it, as there are many experiences that take place here at sunset, if you are willing to see."

Suddenly a roar of Egyptian cowboys came galloping our way. Their leader was carrying our food while the others were supplying the refreshments. As soon as they

Sunset at Giza. (Author's Collection)

reached us, the cowboys opened up the carpets like magic and created a setting fit for kings. They animatedly told me at dusk how they love to round up the horses and then for sport race them across the desert landscape like madmen, creating a sandstorm along the way with their cowboy hats and all. I sat to eat with these amazing people who spoke little English, but their communication was an international language called "smile."

Finally we watched the sun go down on the Pyramids. It doesn't matter how many times I've seen this plateau, it always seems like the first time. The Pyramids will always remain a mystery as long as we question the impossibility of their majesty and the wonder of how they were built with the tools of their time. "Mystery" comes from the Greek word "mien," to close the mouth. When looking at the enigmatic face of the Sphinx as an example, they certainly did.

As darkness came upon us, we wrapped up what was left of the food and made our way back. It was interesting to ride among other camels, donkeys, horses, humans and cars. All fitting the modern environment, all interweaving with each other in an ancient atmosphere that has existed for thousands of years. By exploring these cultures, by riding the path of those who have come before, we become part of that inheritance. I liked that; somehow it expanded my purpose here and reason for my existence in this world. As a small boy, I was fascinated by things I perceived as alien. I always had to touch them, and that way knew they were real. It was a full day and now it was time to go back to the hotel, as tomorrow would begin my journey following the footsteps of the Holy Family along the Nile.

Looking back now at what transpired in Egypt in November of 2010, its revolution, Mubarak's downfall and his house arrest in Sharm el-Sheikh were necessary to bring Egypt into a modern democratic world. The military have taken over and people of the revolution have been imprisoned and tortured. A prosecution spokesman was quoted as saying that the scope of the investigations taking place would include Mubarak and his sons, the crackdown on protesters that killed hundreds of people as well as the corruption allegations into the president's wealth.

I have great memories in Egypt and they will remain with me forever. But who knows where the revolution will end up? In the hands of its people or another leader pretending to be "for the people"? In January of 2012 the first democratic elections took place and the results brought the Muslim Brotherhood into power. Now they celebrate the anniversary of the revolution in Tahrir Square, where it all started. Now we are awaiting the solution for its people's freedom, Arab-style.

The Elgin Marbles

I always imagined that when I saw the Acropolis in Athens for the first time I would run up to the top, to that towering crown of Greece, and visually feast upon the masterpiece at my feet. I had felt like this twice in my life, once in front of the Pyramids in Egypt and now at the Acropolis. It was built on top of this sacred rock during the Golden Age of Pericles between 495–429 BC.

Landing in Greece, home of my ancestors, I grabbed a cab and rushed into Athens. The taxi driver hailed, "There is the Parthenon!" in Greek, and I gazed in its direction but didn't really look it at. This was not how I first wanted to experience it. Not from a distance surrounded by unattractive architecture but whole, in its great splendor, in its full expression, a place where mythical gods resided above the common crowd.

I arrived at my hotel and asked the taxi driver to wait. I registered, dropped off my bags and dashed to the site of my childhood dream.

Crossing the Giza plateau. (Author's Collection)

As I exited the taxi, the driver directed me to the ascent.

I thanked him and proceeded to pace myself up the steep pathway. Below me now was the Theatre of Dionysius with its weathered architecture surrounded by the ancient Agora. What a sight. Worn with such decadence, its life force still exuding its beauty. They did it well in those days, and here I was 2,500 years later and my actor self wanted to race down onto that stage and live in the present by reciting something of the past in Greek. What a great notion.

I raced down to the theatre and climbed onto the stage, oblivious to the tourists in front of me. Wow, I thought, here I am standing with this magnificent ancient backdrop and its auditorium where Euripides' and Homer's tales were performed. And suddenly what came to mind was something Giorgio de Chirico, the Greek-born Italian artist, once said. And so in Greek I spoke his words:

"To become truly immortal, a work of art must escape all human limits; logic and common sense will only interfere. But once these barriers are broken, it will enter the realms of childhood visions and dreams."

The sudden sound of applause from the tourists awakened me out of my reverie. Slightly embarrassed but still a ham, I had no choice but to take a bow. We all had a good laugh, and I continued back up the glorious rock of my childhood dream. Two steps at a time, never looking up, reaching the top I continued through the archway until I could go no further. I looked up and there it was, the Parthenon. It was bigger and greater than I had ever imagined, those amazing columns riddled with wounds of its past history.

When I truly took it all in, I began to sob, which surprised me because rarely in my life have I been that raw and emotional in public. But this time I was realizing a fantasy just as I had at the Pyramids at Giza. Like the past before me I was facing the icon of Greece. My, how it must have looked in its day! But since its inception, the occupation by the Venetians, the Ottomans and the British resulted in these unbelievable scars. That's what wars do: annihilate the face of the conquered.

The 350 years of Ottoman occupation took its toll. They used it as a military fort and fortified it with ammunition. The ceiling and its many statues were destroyed, blown apart or broken down or in most cases looted. Some of its statuary and other artwork considered pagan, particularly idols of gods created in man's image and the display of genitalia, were chopped off and discarded. During the Venetian occupation General Morosini looted some of the larger sculptures. His tackle snapped, and life-size statues of Poseidon and the Horses of Athens Chariot fell over the rock of the Acropolis, plunging forty feet below. The Greek War of

Independence (1821–1833) finally ended the Ottoman rule of Athens, but alas, all of this contributed to its scarring.

As Lord Byron, the great poet, wrote in his "Childe Harold's Pilgrimage":

> Dull is the eye that will not weep too soon,
> Thy wall defaced, thy moldering shrines removed
> By British hands, it had best be behooved
> To guard those relics ne'er to be restored.
> Curst be the hour when from their isle they roved,
> And once again thy hapless bosom gored,
> And snatch'd thy shrinking Gods to Northern climes
> Abhorred!

In 1801, one of the worst offenders, and where controversy still continues today, was the work of a Scotsman named Lord Elgin. He removed many metopes and slabs by hacking off the main structure, sawing and slicing them into sections and causing irreparable damage to the Parthenon. In those ten years it took to bring them down more damage was done than in the rest of its 2,500-year existence. One shipload of marbles on board the British rig *Mentor* was caught in a storm and sank near Kythera Island. It took them two years to bring them back up to the surface. They were eventually bought by the British government and put on display in the British Museum. Even Napoleon put in a bid, and why not? The French and the English were two of the greatest looters of the 19th century. No wonder their museums are full.

I walked around the rock, looking out over Athens where mythical gods perched, taking in all of what was. In those days I had the opportunity to walk through the Parthenon and its hollowed heart. I ran around, my arms outstretched, taking in what great history had lived through this city's center until I got reprimanded by a guard screaming, "Behave yourself."

Meanwhile, I just wanted to dance. How could I explain to him what I was experiencing? My experience was unforgettable and my euphoria came by embracing all I was taught by my parents and my teachers. It was exhilarating. But then its gaping wounds were disturbing.

I then decided to take a quick trip to London to view Elgin's stolen pieces displayed in a country that had no classical age of its own.

As I entered the British Museum I was shocked to witness so many looted artifacts from other cultures, magnificently executed. In my mind they didn't belong there. Finally I found myself in front of what I had come to see, so beautifully displayed by the museum, the enormous sculptured pieces of the Parthenon, looking alive as if they were moving but frozen in time. But that was to the artist's credit. I imagined what they must have looked like in their original habitat, all from one structure. You can't help but be moved.

I remember the emotional reaction of Melina Mercouri, the Greek actress who became the cultural minister of Greece in the 1980s. She turned it into a great performance, standing there in front of the British press, demanding that Greece's majestic icons be returned to her homeland. With that, the tears fell. It was a moving performance filled with Greek tragedy, but her point was made to deaf ears. I had met her in my early years in New York. She was unique and intimidating.

As I stood there, an American tourist made a comment to me about how beautiful the pieces were and by remaining in London they were preserved and protected from the pollution in Athens.

I said to him, "Really? Then you don't know the history of these pieces. These artifacts in London suffered from 19th-century pollution, which persisted until the mid-20th century and were irrevocably damaged by the cleaning methods they used in the 1930s. They were chemically scrubbed which caused the eating away of the original patina."

The American responded with a statement, "Mistakes were made at the time."

"No, it's because it's the largest draw in the museum. Don't talk to me about the pollution in Athens. What if someone stole the Statue of Liberty in New York and you had to visit it in some foreign museum? Would that be upsetting to you? After all, it is your icon." He thought I was overreacting. And so the controversy continues.

So when you go to Greece, Italy, Egypt and China, they exhibit only their history. They didn't have to borrow or steal anyone else's identity.

I read that the Parthenon appears to have been built as a "celebration for the creation of mankind," and fittingly its sculptures and metopes tell its story. Therefore, without them it's not complete. Getting them back to their original historical and cultural environment would allow for fuller understanding and interpretation about what these ancient scholars and artists passed down through wisdom and knowledge and architecture. It's important that people can continue to be reminded of their heritage, how they lived and the standards they held.

The Chinese said: "The spirit of the artist lives through it forever and without it, a culture dies."

The Great Elgin Marbles, British Museum. (Author's Collection)

The Sacrifice, Parthenon. (Author's Collection)

One of the arguments that the British presented was that Greece didn't have a museum large enough to house the Parthenon Marbles. When they did, the British Parliament would re-address their argument. So when the Games were held in Athens for the first time since their inception, their dream was to have the Marbles leave England by train and paraded through European cities, making their final destination in Greece at the Olympic games in 2004.

But, disappointed that the dream didn't take place, Greece decided to build its own museum below the Acropolis. And what a museum it is. Its glass floors reveal parts of ancient Athens below it and what has remained of the magnificent Acropolis artifacts. In June of 2009, the museum opened with dignitaries from all over the world. The British have not budged on their promises, and so Greece is left with empty hands. While they wait and the museum space remains empty, a black ribbon sits above the entrance in mourning of its stolen artifacts.

Kastellorizo

Kastellorizo and its harbor with Turkey in the background. (Author's Collection)

From London I went back to Greece, to the island of Kastellorizo where my ancestors settled in the early 16th century. They migrated from Constantinople (now Istanbul) onto this little rock of an island, a couple of miles from the Turkish coastline.

The name of this island means "the castle with the red plant," which grows wildly over its landscape. The castle belonged to the 14th-century Venetians who inhabited the island. This lovely ruin blends into the rocky terrain overlooking its wonderful harbor where a Greek flag flows freely above the neo-classical houses. At its height, the women of the island would parade along the harbor wearing their best dowry complete with a lace umbrella and "you may look, but don't touch" attitude.

When I was a boy I asked my mother, "Why does Father's mother Kostandina have such a huge nose?"

"It's because she came from a family of wealthy merchants, and feeling important, she always kept her nose in the air. And as we say in Australia — 'a real stuck-up.'"

As I saw it, that nose kept growing, showing off her self-imposed importance. We never liked each other. When the opportunity arose, she would pinch me hard when no one was looking. I somehow seemed offensive to her. Of course, she died an unhappy woman and I was not surprised, her hands were always empty. Not even a rose.

To get to the island I caught a boat in Rhodes, and the experience of the high waves splashing over the deck made the crossing quite rough. We finally entered the harbor of Kastellorizo a bit dazed. Others like me whose ancestors were from this part of Greece began to cry. All the memories of their childhood, the many myths their families had shared with them, had now surfaced and were spilling over, creating what looked more like a Greek tragedy.

I was always told that "When you see the island for the first time, it will be an emotional experience." For me it wasn't. It was a struggle remembering all those traditions enforced upon us, our ancestors coming to Australia and then proceeding to rigidly hand them down in a world different to theirs. And there we clashed; I was rebellious to outmoded concepts. To always behave and be reminded constantly to never ruin the family name. After all, there were sisters that had to be married off eventually, and we couldn't afford to hurt their chances in the arranged-marriage saga. It all seemed so silly now. I rarely saw a happy outcome.

The island looked more like a fairy tale among its ruins with beautifully restored colored houses, all neatly presented on the waterfront as if they were on good behavior. Fishing boats of all colors docked while the fishermen mended their nets. Within its illustrious harbor there were shadows weaving through the battered landscape and not too much light.

As I watched, I reflected upon my youth. I had very little freedom. My father had strict and contradictory rules, and if those rules weren't followed, then his wrath and abuse were revealed. I balked at anything that made me feel like I couldn't breathe. Perhaps that's why open spaces have made me feel so free and alive. My travels in these spaces were part of an education that enhanced my being and most importantly my spirit. It's taken me a lifetime to overcome my father's Victorian attitude. My mother always came to my rescue because my father's frustrations of not fulfilling his destiny and not being able to reach me weighed heavily on my youth.

When we landed I went straight to the spot where my mother and father's families lived, facing the harbor. It was an empty space now after so many wars, fires and earthquakes destroyed a lot of its classic architecture and beautiful landscape. Pity, I would have loved to have sat in that environment where they had been brought up, and maybe that's what I was searching for, something that perhaps would help me understand better who they were and why my father was such a tyrant. Something must have seeded it. Maybe it was because my grandmother never showed any affection to any of us, especially my father, just distance and authority. Those unemotional responses caused a lot of damage.

Soon I found myself facing the school my parents attended in their youth. The magnificent neo-classical architecture hinted at what the island must have really looked like before most of it was destroyed by fires set by the British. Right next to it was the church of St. Kostandinou and Eleni. As I entered the church and lit a candle, the hundreds of icons embraced me, all exuding some kind of revelation, and somehow felt intimidating.

I was able to venture beneath the church where people hid in secret chambers from the enemy. It was claustrophobic so I didn't stay long. I climbed back up into the church and sat in a pew. I took in the smell of the burnt candles and envisioned how they all sat there on a Sunday morning praying to get rid of their guilt, covered up with all those good manners that help carry them through the sermon. An old woman appeared. She was the keeper of the church and lived to keep it pristine. She was one of those people who thought she would definitely go to heaven, having donated her life to the church. She was buoyed by the sounds of those daily chants. A smile came to my face realizing how pure and uncomplicated her needs were.

I prayed for my parents who had passed in 1995. I wish I hadn't waited this long to come here. To be able to call them today and say, "I'm finally here." Or visit with them to witness memories through their eyes. But the cards didn't play it that way, so now I was seeing it through their stories, their voices and how isolated they were on this small island, the farthest from the mainland of Greece. But I do recall my mother telling me that this little spot of earth and its inhabitants were part of the Trojan War in the 14th century BC. She loved that it had such an old rich history.

I climbed the steep slope to the top of the island where I could see the Turkish mainland very clearly some two miles away. The old enemy looked very powerful from a distance. I remembered how the Ottomans spread the worst kind of dominance through a very brutal and sadistic culture. I thought of the Armenian genocide and the control Turkey had over Greece for 350 years. I kept thinking, "Where was God?" Their screams were never heard.

Ancestors' wedding, circa 1929. (Author's Collection)

My great-grandparents, circa 1900. (Author's Collection)

The cliffs of Kastellorizo. (Author's Collection)

I eventually came back down to have an early dinner. Everyone I met was charming. The few restaurateurs tried to hustle me in but I was in no hurry. As I settled at one restaurant a woman approached me who had known my mother very well. "You look so much like her." I smiled and sat at her simple café overlooking the bay.

It was sad when she spoke of my parents and the kind of people they were. My father, who after my success finally accepted me, apparently loved talking about my career. As though his influence was a guiding force. What I really escaped was his lack of embrace. But I shared with those who listened how much my journeys in life made my father feel that some part of him succeeded through his son. What the hell, it changed him late in life for the better. I know that if parents don't want you to go beyond them in fear of losing you, you have to make a shift, leave them behind and be true to your own self. Then they will be able to see through the maze when success follows you. As Milton Katselas used to say to me, "Out-create them." And by having success, it broadened their vision and certainly mine. And so I finally came to peace with myself, and was able to let my father go, gracefully.

The next morning at dawn, I caught a small boat to take me to the Grotto. As I stepped onto the boat my driver greeted me. Before long we motored out and I could see the clarity of the water below where my father as a young man had gone diving, bringing up hundreds of sea urchins and sponges in small nets. It's just phenomenal what we remember.

A short while later we traveled around the rock and observed its historic remains. I was reminded what history had passed by these monuments. Age-old battles, domination by the Greeks, to the Crusaders, Turks, Italians, French and finally back to the Greeks. We had left early in the morning because when the tide is high the Grotto disappears. We arrived and entered the cave's narrow entrance, and there was that water, so blue it almost appeared artificial. It was aquamarine. So beautiful, I dove in and felt the silky water that my father had described when he was having one of his good days. The light piercing through the cave created a magical atmosphere. I kept thinking how my parents had swum here in their youth. And now here I was, swimming in their memories.

I eventually climbed back into the boat and headed toward the hotel. At dusk I began to walk along the different paths and take in the symmetry of this land and how many of its inhabitants lost their fortunes during the early 20th century and made their way to America and Australia. I grew up believing that we were part of an enormous heritage of royal connections, and that if you were not from Kazzie (the nickname of the island) you were not a Greek, but a foreigner. All this self-importance about the kind of history you came from and the lifetime it took to remove its imprint. But I learned to understand it better as I grew older and my eyes became clearer.

I heard a flute playing in the distance and finally spotted a shepherd rounding up his goats and sheep at the bottom of the hill. Not much has changed here, unlike America where every day brings change and little time to realize success. It was a serene scene. I imagined holding my father and mother's hands and leading them up the hill, being young again when there was time to laugh and enjoy afternoon Greek coffee where an old woman would read your fortune.

But they have gone now.

As the sun took its leave beyond the horizon, I felt them slip out of my hands and disappear to wherever that next stage of life may be. I miss them dearly — and for the first time realized how difficult it was for them to leave this tiny paradise and venture to an Anglo country where they put their pride aside to start at the bottom, doing labor work where little fantasy was left for them in that great and newly developed country called Australia.

I left the following day having a better sense of my parents by visiting their place of birth and the stories that unfolded when I was young. Their little Kastellorizo with its remains, its old and new inhabitants, and those who left, brought their

NeoClassical house on Kastellorizo. (Author's Collection)

children back to witness their heritage and by doing so kept their culture alive. As the boat was pulling away I couldn't help but quietly sing a melody that my family had taught me, with the sound of my mother playing the mandolin echoing in my mind. A smile warmed my face as I felt the magic that only faraway places can give you, especially when you have connected to your past and you shift into new beginnings. It's as if the island had been a myth. My quest of exploring it was fulfilled by being there in the present and letting go of the outmoded thoughts. Kastellorizo had now become real.

It seems that all the journeys I have taken were places to hide, to forget, to escape, and eventually discover some meaning hidden behind the walls I chose to climb. And by having climbed over them and embracing the mystery that was waiting to be revealed, dangerous or not, it helped me weave a fabric that I would wear for the rest of my life, and in the end bring me closer to the God that lives through me.

> But do not hurry the voyage at all.
> It is better to let it last for many years;
> Ithaca has given you the beautiful voyage.
>
> Wise as you have become, with so much experience,
> You must already have understood what Ithacas mean.

—Cavafy

Top to Bottom:

My grandparents, George and Polexeni Kiossoglou.

My cousins with Uncle Bill and Grandfather George in humble times.

Mum, left, and Uncle Bill during early 1940s.

Opposite page, clockwise from top:

Arriving home to family and relatives.

My parents in my Los Angeles home.

My sister Connie and Mum.

Crown St. Primary School in Sydney, where it all began.